PULLIN' CHAINS
STAY YOUR BUTT OUT OF PRISON

MICHAEL VON
PENNINGTON-DEVINE

www.facebook.com/michaelpenningtondevine
www.twitter.com/miamimikedevine
www.linkedin.com/miamimikedevine

The opinions expressed in this manuscript are solely the opinions of the author and do not represent the opinions or thoughts of the publisher. The author has represented and warranted full ownership and/or legal right to publish all the materials in this book.

Pullin' Chains
Stay Your Butt Out of Prison
All Rights Reserved.
Copyright © 2013 Michael Von Pennington-Devine
v2.0

2005 Department of Justice Report: articles.cnn.com/2002-10-31/us/tulsa.shooting_1_security

Scripture quotations marked (NIV) are taken from the Holy Bible, New International Version®, NIV®. Copyright © 1973, 1978, 1984, 1985, 2011 by Biblica, Inc.™ Used by permission of Zondervan. All rights reserved worldwide. www.zondervan.com The "NIV" and "New International Version" are trademarks registered in the United States Patent and Trademark Office by Biblica, Inc.™

Cover Design by Thomas E. Lockhart .
Cover Image James Rowe . All rights reserved - used with permission.

This book may not be reproduced, transmitted, or stored in whole or in part by any means, including graphic, electronic, or mechanical without the express written consent of the publisher except in the case of brief quotations embodied in critical articles and reviews.

Pennington Communications, Inc.

ISBN: 978-0-578-12447-6

Library of Congress Control Number: 2013909193

PRINTED IN THE UNITED STATES OF AMERICA

Notice of Verifiable Facts Disclaimer

This is a true story based on public record and all steps have been taken to ensure every aspect of this story is true and that any misrepresentation was unintentional describes an actual occurrence or event and experience the author had {Narrative, biography} personal reflections providing a certain amount of passion or emotional depth to the work. To the best of our ability to remember the story is true and every effort was made to contact those involved.

Notice in 2013-2016

I'd like to get this book out to as many people as possible, specifically those who are incarcerated in our prisons and jails. Millions are presently incarcerated in prisons, on probation, or on parole in America. This does not include those locked up in more than 33,000 local city jails. If you feel led to help me print more books, please call me at 305 767 6217, write us or email us at: pcofc1@yahoo.com

*He brought them out of darkness,
the utter darkness,
and broke away their chains.*

– Psalms 107:14 (NIV)

Dedicated to

Both of my parents Maerene C. Newton- Pennington and Deacon Charles Russell Pennington for dealing me the cards I was dealt so that I could be who God intended for me to be to the rest of the world a miracle, my precious children the late- Devon Scooter T. Sutton, Michael Jr., and Destiny, David, Kelli and Guy. Last but not least to all of the boys and girls, men and women like Mr. Malcolm Kelley, who read this book and find your strength to go on and win in this life through Christ. To everybody else stay your butt out of prison!!!!

Thanks for your assistance with this project and inspiration.

Big Frank Alexander former Bodyguard of Tupac Shakur may you both R.I.P.

Middle picture from Tulsa, Oklahoma Tour of Public Schools and Job Corp.

Contents

Foreword i
Acknowledgements ix
Preface xv
Introduction xix

1. May My Livin' Never Be in Vain 1
2. Charged 6
3. Marriage on the Rocks, Please! 10
4. Lord, Help Me! 12
5. Tellin' It Like It Is: Let Me Clear My Throat 16
6. Green Mile: The Movie 19
7. Everybody's Daddy 21
8. Okay, Who Is Mr. Mike? 26
9. Nobody Listening 28
10. Taking Our Child 32
11. Gospel Music Stellar Awards 34
12. Get Involved 36
13. Bout It, Bout It 41
14. 2001 47
15. North Point 51

16. VIP Limo 57
17. Out on Bail 59
18. Attempted Murder Was the Case 62
19. The Night Aalyiah Died 63
20. 3 Strikes 65
21. D.A. Carl Funderburk and Judge Linda Morrissey 66
22. What Law Changed? CLEET ! TITLE 21 § 1290.1 68
23. M.T.S. 71
24. Black Man's University 73
25. She Was Right 75
26. Rodeo Ryde and Killing Judges 77
27. Vacation vs. State Property 81
28. Them, You, and Me: Public View of Prison(s) 83
29. The Food, Cells, Smells, and Safety 85
30. Don't Drop the Soap 87
31. Cutting Hair and Mental Test 88
32. Introduction to Me 91
33. All Eyes on Me: Life File 92
34. Em' O.G. Now 94
35. Bo Jangling 97
36. Historical University Research 99
37. In Conclusion 106

About the Author 111
Where Is the Author Today? 113
Strong, Empowering Scripture(s) 115
"All Inmates Should Be Given a Second Chance." 123
Recommended Reading List 127
The Lord Reigns 141

Foreword

This book is a long time coming! This is a must read in really understanding the prison system. You will understand that (The system is not your friend!) and that it wants you for its money machine when you can't get right in regular society. Thank you, Michael for blessing us with this book. Let's get the word out. STAY YOUR BUTT OUT OF PRISON!!!

– Thomas E. Lockhart III,
Colorado Department Correctional Staff

I've been on the battlefield in the streets with these kids for the last 29 years known as The Rev. I've watched what drugs, gangs and prison does to a community. I feel like Moses in the latter years. I've seen so much death and I am feeling this book of hope. I see young brothers like Brother Mike Pennington-Devine as the new Joshua's of our time as I pass the torch on to this 'hip hop intellectual-author and pastor'. I have been there done that, and faced serious consequences in my past and was pardoned. This book you are reading is what has become of a young brother listening and watching, my actions up close, while finding his own true story of redemption and hope and a bright future. I am claiming that his words are going to convict you as a reader.

– The Reverend Leon Kelly,
*Pastor of Open Door Youth Gang Alternative
and Director of Flippin' the Script
Colorado Department of Corrections Parole*

It should awaken the awareness and the lives of individuals that may have experienced similar things contained in this book. Through his testimony it clearly shows that through God all things are possible. This book *Pullin Chains* proves we can all live as over comer's in life.

Pullin' Chains

*Caught in a whirlwind
Enticed by what came easy
Ensnared by my own actions
Sentenced to do time
Committer of crimes
No rhyme or reason
Ones own self destruction
Lost focus of what was rational
Blinded by the temporal
Led by freshly gain through it all
remaining sane in these streets
ain't no game it's a shame how
we are herded away as chattel
buried in a system that doesn't*

care forgotten by many
remembered by none
as I pull these chains.

– **Prophetess Leah M. Kelley**

The Blessing of Answered Prayer

I was a big fan of 2 Live Crew and when Mike made his break from the underground of Miami we met at my home church in Philly. I had them all on my prayer list with hopes of their change in the Lord. Over the years, I have watched this brother evolve and survive on nothing but his faith to get to this day. This book *"Pullin Chains"* is a true testimony to that journey.

– **TSgt Carolyn G. Keys,**
Commander Support Staff (CSS)Pennsylvania Air National Guard

It is a pleasure to write this forward for Pastor Mike Pennington-Devine. It is imperative to keep our youth in the forefront of our minds as we go about our daily lives. There are too many youth as well as adults who are suffering at the hands of the enemy (Satan) because they do not understand their purpose in life. God has given us all divine purpose for this life and going to prison is not one of them. Each one of us must seek the Lord's guidance and look to Him for answers, truths and deliverance just as Pastor Mike did. It was Christ who taught him how to stay his butt out of prison. You can learn the Lord's ways for your life too. I understand some people may say I don't believe in God. What have God done for me? If God is real, why is my life the way it is? The fact of the matter is you have not been looking in the right places. If you seek the Lord, Jesus Christ with all of your heart and mind you will find his presence and experience his love for you. You are not an outcast neither the black sheep of the family. You were created in the expressed image of God. You are powerful and creative just like our heavenly Father. Given an opportunity, you will find yourself just like Him. Although you may not acknowledge Him now, you are like him in many ways. This book *"Pullin Chains"* will give you some insights on how to keep yourself from becoming confined inside of the prison walls. You will learn what it takes to put your life back on the right path and how to identify who you really are. Pastor Mike's life experience will give you hope in knowing that it's not how you start but how you finish. Success has always been in your hands. The choices you make today will certainly affect your tomorrow. Choose this day whom you will serve (Christ or Satan) and you will choose the path of how successful or unsuccessful you will become both now and in the future. Whom the Lord has set free is free indeed. Our heavenly Father wants to free your mind, body, soul and spirit today. Don't become what someone else wants you to become. Become who you were predestined by God to become before you were in your mother's womb. You are "fearfully and wonderfully made" (Psalm 139:14, KJV). Pastor Mike, I want to thank you for deciding to take a stand for righteousness and allowing God to use you to your fullest potential. Your testimony of your life's trials and triumphs will help many others who are bonded by chains to be set free.

– **Shannon Walton**,
Ambassador for Christ

As a longtime friend of Mike Pennington-Devine a.k.a. "Miami Mike D" I have had the pleasure of witnessing one of the biggest hearts for the success of kids, live and in action... and what you're going to get from his wonderfully articulated work *"Pullin Chains"* is a literary testimony of an inspirational life that's going to challenge and encourage young and old, to "stay your butt out of prison."

– Victor Nellum,
Youth and Young Adult Pastor, Anchor Of Hope Church

You are about to witness a personal journey of a new social movement in America where our young brothers are taking a stand in society. Pastor Mike was a part of the Security team we relied on at North Pointe Business Center for a few years. Often I'd spend a few times engaging in powerful conversations with him about neighborhood conditions and what we were witnessing. This book focuses on fighting back against the multileveled assault on the poor and vulnerable who struggle through the breakdown in the system. Just picture how this author shows concern for his fellow man, especially the conditions of our youth going to prison. I assessed his whole drama he faced with him before his devastating incarceration. I was limited in assisting him. He was in too deep. Invaluable and timely of the truth-telling at all of us for what we call justice in America. Join him in his crusade to reach as many as he can through this writing of *"Pullin' Chains"*.

– Joe Williams,
Former City Councilmen & 100 Black Men of Tulsa, OK

Like the Bible, this is a must read for those who want a guide to how we being troubled by injustice as Christians in the faith fought back in Tulsa. I was there with him as the story unfolded. Racism is still real with a badge striking at our freedom as blacks. I praise Pastor Mike for allowing God to use him mightily. We transformed the facility and I know this author is genuine about touching lives through his music and now this book "Pullin Chains".

– **Pastor McFranklin Alexander**

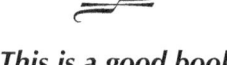

This is a good book

Taught each other right from the start to be color blind and broke society's racial barriers that even adults could not begin to understand. Friendship, loyalty and brotherhood, we are family.

If it wasn't for Pastor Mike, I would not be the Man, Father, Husband, I am today. If it wasn't for P-man/Devine, I would not be part of the Hip Hop culture that he introduced me to.

– **Thomas *"Demo52 of ATKM Crew"* McMillan,**
WSD-Juvenile Services Center

Masterpiece!!!!

All through my experience as a weekly newspaper publisher, bank teller, real estate broker, insurance agent, and 14 years in the Oklahoma State House of Representatives and

State Senate, then 23 years teaching with Department of Corrections, I've thought "Helping People Is Our Business." Mike Pennington-Devine is one of my most successful students from the Jim E. Hamilton Correction Center in Hodgen, Ok. I'm thrilled to wish him great success in his life and literary effort. His sharing of this work to **help others** will bless many and it certainly does give us all the thought that we can be in the **Salvage Business.** A human life would be a terrible thing to waste.

– Mr. Joe Johnson,

Retired Oklahoma Congressmen &
Retired Oklahoma Department of Corrections,
Director of New Direction Program

Acknowledgements

You know and I know that J to E to the SUS is so real to me so I give praise and honor to HIM. There are so many who were there with me through the thick, slim and thin, I wanted to thank you: For all her hard work at BluestockingInk, Cynthia Roby words are not enough to say how you have touched this book with your anointing to do what you do. I prayed and God sent me Jerry Banks and the whole team at Outskirts, we family from now on in Parker, CO., My precious and gentle spirit wife Pamela N. Pennington, Malcolm & Weorgia, Jessica Newton, Lil' Joy, Katheleen, Donte', Terrell and LaTeisha, Thomas & Latrice Lockhart, Chris & Cedric Bobo, Julia Pennington-Gilchrist, Gino & Elaine Scott, Robert and GeGe Levison, Anthony, Paulette, Mrs. Kattie Pennington and daddy, Shawnadre Crews, Patrick Ingle, Lenzy Blake, all of my law and writing professors at MCC- Rochester, NY and CCD- Denver, CO; Pastor Billy & Cynthia Thompson, Arnel Moe zart Thompson, Bishop Dennis Jackson, Sr., James G. Spady for all the long talks, books and lessons, Jerald January for writing a book I could read in one night and it changed my life when I needed it " a messed up ride and a dressed up walk, Victor & Que Nellum & kids, RIP- Vince Guillory of Compassion, Tommy Moore, Pastor Robert Woolfolk, Pastor Kenneth Roberts, Pastor Michael & Brenda Walker, DeVaughn & Retina Renee Gray, Grandma Freda & Keith Gray (The Gray family), Pastor Stephen E. Broden & The Fair Park Bible Fellowship Church family, Resi (Sacred) Muse & family, Jose Phil Tavernier (faisal), Dr.Chedda- Jerome Singleton & Fila Phil, Big Roc Rick Williams & family, Big Frank Alexander, RIP-Tupac Shakur, RIP- Pamela Williams and Traci Jones-Blackwell, gone too soon also my other sister Vicki Newton, Cheryl Mizell (power to the people) we recorded my first gospel rap tracks in your place in the USA-Flea Market, Han Soul, Da'Truth and Tha Lord's Ambassador, Thelma Warren & Monty Davis, Keita Andrews, Sherri & Sheila Prince, Coach Bill McCartney & Kristy, Floyd & Regina Jackson, Aaron & Sonya Henderson, Rev. Kenneth Dupree, Clarence Shuler, Melanie Diggs, Bishop Brian Keith Williams & Donna, Bishop Jones, Linda & Selwyn Ray, Susan & Leo Keily, Nicky Cruz, DCP-Beanie Tucker & LG WISE, 2G'z-Gospel Gangstaz, Oscar & Linda Roan, Smokey John Reaves, RIP-Gloria Reaves, Al Bryant & Family, RIP-Claudette Bryant, Rudy, Darrin & Naomi Smith, Joe Williams@ONG & Staff, Pastor Lewis Bumpers, Pastor Alvin Simpkins & family, Elder David & Beatrice Shaw, Rebecca Jimerson, Rodney Gray, Mendenhall Bible Church, Pastor El Thighpen, Brother Jones, John Perkins, Minister Chris (Brother Reg) Green from Boyz N The HOOD Movie, Carol Parnell-Smith, Sarah, Molly, Brent & Kathy Hatch, Promise Dixon, Theodora, Reggie, Marvin Chatman, Margo Lewis, Bishop Earthquake Kelley, Andre Crouch, Michelle James & family, Gethsemane Missionary Baptist Church, TJ Milan & family, NaTasha Frasier- Holland, Joe Erhmann- Inside Out, Denver Institute of Urban Studies(DIUS), Patricia Ashton & family, CJ- Jacobs & family, Kevin Matthews, RIP- Min. George

Lopez, Bennie Wright, Jr., Anita, Christopher, Victoria & Bernard Wright, Sr., George Ronnie Lyons, RIP- Gloria Lyons, Mother King, Cleo Harris, Min. Mike Hill & family, Min. Alvin Muhammad, Carol Smith, Willard & Lucille Thierry, Creative T's & Uncle Ben Nelson, Orlando Jasper, Jerry Jarvis, Pastor Felicia Whipple, Irvin Profit, Quincy & Mario Roans, Pastor Age & Officer Flo Sandavol, James & Jaketa Rowe, Turner L. Goodrum, Greenwood Pharmacy, RIP- Dr. Gary R. Davis, Jesse Jackson,Sr, and Congressman Jesse Jackson, Jr., Min. Tony Knolls, Lonnie Tolbert, Jesus People Ministries, RIP Bishop Isaiah Williams, Tom McCartney, Ulysses G., Joseph Jennings, Dr. Fairest Hill, Pastor Jerry Acosta, Lawrence Doc Reed, Philippe@ The Barbershop, Sgt. Carolyn Keys & family, Sgt. Shannon Walton, Cynthia Hodge, all of the people from all the schools I attended and cities I've lived in, OCBF-family in Dallas, C/O 1985 Youth Group of OCBF, Dr. Tony Evans, Kirk Franklin, Katrine & James Taylor, Norman & Dee Dee Jones, Lowe Barry & all other SFC- Soldiers For Christ, Charles & Deborah McCampbell & family, Min. Vincent Spann of Overtown, Min.Vincent Black of Carver Ranches, Pastor Victor T. Curry & family, all my relatives near and far like Uncle Sunny Murray in Paris, Uncle Connie Turner in Brazil, Dewey Patterson, Joe Johnson, Mary Jenkins & family, Jesse Fields, Ole Pete Key & family, Kirk Whalum, Nichol Mullen, Lady J(wherever you are in NE), Michael Chatman, Jonnette Newton, Fernisha Allen-Spann & Big Donald Spann, Melvin Bratton & the whole family, Pee Wee The DJ from Chicago, Carla Sanders, Darrin McCarter, Knolly Williams, MC Hammer & Family, Mark Klosterman,Sandra Murray, Lisa M. Bradley, Beverly D. Smith, Deborah Wilson, Lucinda Thierry Riles, Tania Smith, Renee, Brandon, Colin, Na Na Bordeaux & family, James Barnett, Leonard Pitts, MVP, Divine Flava, Les Brown, RIP- Zig Ziglar, Tom Leding, Ricardo Flo & Platinum

Soul, Joseph Patrick Hap McMullen, Lagaya Allen Kwame, Luther Uncle Luke Campbell, Chris Wong Won (Fresh Kid Ice), Brother Marquis Ross, Pastor Fred Lynch, RIP-Keith Marcel Cruel, Carlton Wright a true Miami Central Rocket like me, Paula Davis, Paula Nelson, Sir Walter Scott III, Mr. Charlie Wilson for asking me to kick it and pray with the GAP BAND back stage in Tulsa, Rodney Tucker - Jones, Sheryce Resi (Sacred)Muse, MacFranklin Alexander, Mr. Kurtis Blow(Minister), Rev Run, Dr. Cornel West, Chuck D, Professor Griff, The Planet Walker, Marvelous JP(Jerry Parker), Chico the Leo (Bernard Veargis), Sheryl, Baby Ced, Sam, G I- Joe and all of The Ghetto Style & Pit Bull DJ's, Jordace- JDC, Galilee 3:16 aka Will & Rodney Paytee, Sabrina & Min. Jeremy Veargis, Lady Jane Carnegie- Tolliver, Success Kidz, Inc, Brenda Faye & Dee Dee Moncrief, Jasmine Peters & family, Dr. Tina Dupree(The Chicken Lady from Down South), Mrs. Rose', Baron and Kevin Hallum. La Tonia and Darren, Kenny & Keith King, Apelle King & family,Minister Wayne Cherry, Pastor Howard Roberts, AJ Wright, Veronica Wade, Venus Caldwell, Reggie Pierre (Nice & Wild), Pennie Munlin-Williams, Abby Bivins & family, Janeen Howard & family, Muhammad Ali (on our Juvenile Prison Tour had me crying, You're The Greatest!), RIP- Ofc. Roy Tennyson, Rochell LeBlanc Taylor, Ray McCampbell,(At Summer camp you kept my head in the word) Major Greene & family, Audrey Brown, Lesli, Tasha, Stephanie, Greg McNeal and our whole youth group of OCBF, Karen Jackson(ya family always), Willie Jackson, Jr., Fekeya and all of my Scott Lake R.R.P.-Posse', Brother Roach, The Late Charles Smith, Janice and Lisa Smith, Karen K. Jones(family), Timothy Carter, Richard CNOTEX- Wilson, Katerine Frater-Dowdy, Deirdra Deas, Tangela Rolle, Greg- Kwame Rodgers, LaVena & Family, Cookie & Demi Rodriguez, RIP-Danny D-Boy Rodriguez, Leah Kelley & family (This book was originally dedicated to your son Malcolm Kelley as promised glad you back home from your bid brah. Stay ya butt out!)

All my nieces Aisha Allen, Konshawnia, Ebuni, Tiffany Roberts, Whitney Kenyatta Roberts and nephews Farnell Newton, lil'Donald Spann and Troy Newton, Kieta Kwame Allen & family, my cousins Dana & David Turner, lil Devon Scooter Sutton, Jr., LaQuana Arnold, RIP- Devon Scooter Sutton, Sr., Weorgia(Ygee) & Dr. H. Malcolm Newton, Mercedes Johnson. RIP- P Man Sam Ferguson (Silvasteen), Barry Small & family, RIP- Joe Small. Kevin, Asha & Karla Patrick, all my family attorneys like Evan Ostfeld

Preface

1 Corinthians 15:10 is where Apostle Paul says, "But by the grace of God I am what I am". I learned as a child in my neighborhood what my role would be in the body of Christ, my particular gifts, and the specific burden God put on my heart to serve Him. I was very young when I experienced witnessing death and my mother treating severe gunshot wounds made me face the hard truth that you can't save everyone all the time. The challenges of this lesson led to stressful experiences like being sent to prison and for me to write this book is much therapy. As I learned what being a child of God really meant I also learned that a well-read bible is a sign of a well-fed soul. I thank my dear God above so much for giving me a second chance today to make a difference with my life and experiences. May the Lord help those hurting deep down inside right now and guide them and give them strength as a result of this book. I heard it said, "I may not be who I ought to be. I know I'm not all that I want to be. But I've come a long way from who I use to be Inmate number 406740 and I won't give up on becoming what I know I can be. So, I want to encourage the reader to live through your experiences,

embrace all mistakes for they will teach you life's lesson. I hope this book fires you UP because for me these moments are my memories that make them worth remembering with a grateful heart. I'm talking to you! Don't look back; you're not going that way, Pullin' Chains. You are exactly where you need to be. You can survive anything.

"I will put my spirit in you and you will live." *Ezekiel 37:14a* (NIV) Game on!

Thanks to all Inmates and Staff

The Thirteenth Amendment to the United States Constitution officially abolished and continues to prohibit slavery and involuntary servitude except as punishment for a crime. It was passed by the U.S. Senate on April 8, 1864, the House on January 31, 1865, and adopted on December 6, 1865. It was then declared in the proclamation by Secretary of State William H. Seward on December 18. It was the first of the Reconstruction Amendments

STAY OUT OF PRISON
A NEW DIRECTION

A prison (from the Old French prisoun) is a place in which people are physically confined and usually deprived of a range of personal freedoms. Other terms are penitentiary, correctional facility, and jail. Source: The Wiktionary, the free dictionary online.

The United States has the highest documented incarceration rate in the world. The U.S. incarceration rate on June 30, 2009 was 748 inmates per 100,000 U.S. residents, or 0.75%. The United States also has the highest total documented prison and jail population in the world. According to the U.S. Bureau of Justice Statistics (BJS) 7,225,800 people at yearend 2009 were on probation, in jail or prison, or on parole—about 3.1% of adults in the U.S. resident population, or 1 in every 32 adults. As of the yearend 2011, 6.98 million people were incarcerated in U.S. prisons and jails. That's ONE IN 34 U.S. ADULTS UNDER CORRECTIONAL SUPERVISION IN 2011.

Introduction

As a child, I was captured by the images of 60's and 70's television. I remember sitting in front of the television set, a device at which some undetermined time had become my babysitter, engrossed in popular shows such as Captain Kangaroo and the Skipper Chuck Show. Both were filmed in my hometown, Miami. Similarly, Flipper was filmed at The Miami Seaqarium, in Flipper's Lagoon across the Key Biscayne / Rickenbacker Bridge from Downtown Miami just minutes from my home in Overtown. This was a sign that there was more to life than what we were experiencing prior to desegregation on Second Avenue. We stayed in the house a lot; outside was not safe. My mom kept a hammer near the door or on the refrigerator, and a gun in the drawer. I believe that I fired that gun and killed our poor little caged bird. The bullet went over my mom's headboard while she was asleep. Bang! This was one of my introductions to guns. Public Broadcasting System (PBS) productions of Sesame Street, The Electric Company and ZOOM were also big hits on my television. I also found Spider-Man, Bill Cosby, and certain other characters appealing. They almost looked like (skin color or race) but were not from my environment. I can admit this did give me a false sense of reality as a young black child. My emotions were everywhere since I witnessed that man killed or the other person who got pot ash thrown on him. I can never forget him running and screaming. His clothes were on fire as was his face. All I ever knew back then was one or two streets that held nightclubs and businesses and hustlers. Before the highway came and our area was demolished, blacks weren't allowed out of their communities or on Miami Beach after sunset. These shows may have meant something different for my siblings. I was too young to remember much else.

Popular music from singers of the day such as Little Richard, Otis Redding, Sam Cooke, Bill Withers, Aretha Franklin, Johnnie Taylor, or Florida Boy Ray Charles blared from radios and jukeboxes in Dave's Bar and other local family owned establishments along Northwest Second Avenue in Overtown such as Sir John Hotel, The Mary Elizabeth Hotel, The Night Beat, The Rockland Palace and places my dad worked, the Island Club, was a huge scene dubbed The Strip. I live on it baby!

I later watched the movie Dummy with LeVar Burton, whom I recognized from Sesame Street. It was his role in the film that placed a strong fear in my mind about where committing crimes could lead. My mother's male friends often offered advice from their own lives experiences, and whether I could relate at the time was of no concern to them. I don't remember much of what they warned about. I know being a gangster, hustling, and going to prison were stories and warnings to me. Thank you, Sunny Red for those choice words.

These same people, my mother's friends, drove a line of Cadillac cars while rushing me to Jackson Memorial Hospital when I chopped off my right index finger with my bicycle chain. My brother Gino's birthday party was halted as everyone surrounded me. Iron Man, who attended the party, went for his bolt cutter and freed what was left of my tiny digit.

In the movie, Dummy, Burton played deaf-mute. Cared for by his older brother until he came of age, he was later falsely accused, booked, and sentenced for raping and killing a white prostitute. Unfortunately, he had no defense or ability to communicate. Thus he was found guilty and sentenced to prison where he was beaten, raped, and eventually released. The case remained under investigation, and it was later proven that Burton's character had no involvement in the crime. But it was too late. The mental and physical damage had been done. Events such as this have taken place in our society since the day slavery ended.

Abraham Lincoln issued the Emancipation Proclamation on Jan. 1, 1863 as the nation approached its third year of civil war. The proclamation declared "that all persons held as slaves" within the rebellious states "are, and henceforward shall be free." And that's when the endless construction of prisons began. I knew that I never wanted to be sentenced to prison, ever!

My goal is to one day be of greater help to those incarcerated in U.S. prisons. When my ministry began its national expansion it received a great deal of attention from the press. I was volunteering as well as performing weekly in Miami-Dade County jails and Florida's state prisons. Joe Smalls, my Jewish godfather, and other locals who did time in Clyde Killens' pool hall always told me: "You'll be the one to go tell ole' Pharaoh, let my people go!" They often spoke over me in that context. I often ignored them. Whatever they witnessed in my character wasn't important to me at the time. I witnessed many things while there: how grown men couldn't stop hustling, making fast money, and how they were locked out of society because they held a prison record. "Never be like us, kid! Forget the rings, diamonds, cars, and clothes. Do better than this!" they warned.

All of those men planted seeds in my mind that I didn't understand for most of my life, at least until it became necessary. I salute the countless people who took the time out to impart wisdom into my life. It may often appear that I am bragging or idol worshiping, but kept in the proper perspective, I've always felt compelled to give credit where credit is due. It is my prayer that as you read through these pages, you will not only thank the Lord on High, Jesus Christ, but that you take what you can from it and pass it on to others that might come to see the light. I've witnessed young men, specifically those in prison, cry when they learned that what I share of my experiences isn't simply a jailhouse lie but documented facts. Thank you for taking the time to not see the privileges I was afforded, but how the favor and power of God has stayed upon my life.

A Hustler, a Pimp, a Gangsta

"Don't go to prison. Don't get in trouble, Mike."

Over the years I have taken part in several media interviews that focused on how I grew up and the people I grew up around. These interviews oftentimes portrayed my life and those in it as unfavorable ghetto-stapled stereotypes. My life began to change during middle school. Friends were being killed around me. William Brown, a black belt, was first among them killed in a street fight with a baseball bat, and Derrick, aka Mean Machine, died at the Northwest Boys

Club swimming in the lake that's behind the Silver Blue Lakes Apartments, where I lived. Then a close family friend little Rena was stabbed and killed in Fort Lauderdale after being stalked by a man who was crazy. My brother Malcolm was affected by her death too. He came home from Philly while in college and met Rena, who was a beautiful sister staying at our house one weekend. We learned of her tragic death over the news one day. Later on, The Miami Herald published my photograph from the Westview Middle School Career Day Event as I asked the Southern Bell worker questions about a career in communications. Countless television and radio features have followed me throughout my life because I was never afraid to communicate. I've learned the difference between talking to people and the ability to have your own voice. I had to express myself.

I have never been afraid to tell the truth. I have never had the opportunity to express how I was getting real-life Black-man survival lessons from the people in my neighborhood. They'd say: "Do what I say, not as I do." Their lifestyles were duplicitous: they lived their own brand of life surviving by the code of the streets, yet dropped jewels about the real side of things to which I was attracted—bling, fabulousness, and perceived success. This is where I grew up: Overtown in the seventies.

Clyde Killens

Clyde Killens, a local resident and entertainment promoter, was primarily responsible for bringing black entertainers, who were allowed to perform in the clubs on Miami Beach but not stay in the hotels, came to Overtown's Lyric Theater and "Little Broadway." Little Broadway's roster of stars featured performers such as Count Basie, Sam Cooke, Aretha Franklin, The Ink Spots, B.B. King, Patti LaBelle, Ella Fitzgerald, Redd

Foxx, and Mary Wells. Tourists of all races alongside locals enjoyed the area's vibrancy. Overtown was a place known for its nightly entertainment, exotic restaurants and active churches. Celebrities such as Count Basie, Ella Fitzgerald, Cab Calloway, Josephine Baker, Billy Holiday, Nat King Cole, and Aretha Franklin frequented the area. Many other artists performed year round at Sir John Hotel, Mary Elizabeth Hotel, the Lyric Theater, and other Overtown establishments. Additionally, prominent Blacks such as W. E. B. Du Bois, Zora Neale Hurston, Joe Louis, and Jackie Robinson stayed in Overtown while vacationing in Miami.

Mr. Clyde Killens was my landlord when we had an apartment over the pool hall. I lived in Overtown, the so-called "Little Black Harlem of the South." I met enough men who likely do not believe I have ever heard them at all(what they were saying). I have read articles in the city's archives, news clips; viewed photographs that confirmed Killens' involvements. All of these things confirmed the things I had seen and known about our former landlord.

Coming of Age

Despite my age, the movie DUMMIE helped me to visualize the words and expressions of others until I reached the eighth or ninth grade. This was during the time one of our close family friends, Vernon, was killed. The detectives arrived at our front door in Silver Blue Lakes with the news. Vernon, an old gangster, was shot in the head while sitting in the back of a limousine. He was then thrown out the door and left to die in the streets of Overtown. He remained in a coma for a short time. The police could barely make out the names of me and my sister, which he uttered while in distress as his next to kin. This was a manly man. He used to rob banks but later move to Canada, so I am told. We used to have navy bags of money in our house and he would make sure each morning before school that we had whatever we needed: staples such as cereal and milk. I felt a deep-seated anger and lost respect for him because men searching for him with shotguns had started knocking on our door prior to his murder.

I ran errands for all types of people. Some were men, both straight and gay, from prison chain gangs. I recalled this with the help of my biological father, Charles Russell Pennington. There were things that when planning to write this book, I just didn't understand. There were so many people that outlived my mother and continued to encourage me as an adult in church ministry as well. Frank Skip Andrews, like my mom, had strong faith in the streets. Whether they were straight, crooked, or gay, they were protective and honest with me about life, specifically when dealing in the music business and entertainment circles. Few knew how informed and guarded I was in the community back in the day. As a child, they respected my mother, and toward me were polite and kind. I knew when someone did them wrong, as I was given the signal to clear the area. Danger was thick all around. Knives, machetes, guns, and curse words were all signs for me to pull up a nose-bleed seat and pay close attention to some real butt kicking. My hope is that you will now do the same. Pay attention!

My brother Gino, in tears, recently brought up our childhood during a telephone conversation: "We spent a lot of our lives getting over the past sins of others and trying to correct (heal) the mistakes." Running from generational curses is very real to me. I also recognized that I had to reach back to the solutions that were good, then and now, for a new direction.

On weekends, I stayed with a close cousin, Tommy McMillan and his mom Karen. I later underwent middle-class experiences to defuse many of the traumas faced. Between my cousin's home on the weekend and then exiting Florida for Texas with the F.B.I. hot on my trail, life was wild. We had a long-distance credit card scheme; Jamaicans were notorious in business of selling card numbers. I only learned about the law enforcement and other things I was busted about from my brother Malcolm. Attending private school, and especially church, gave my life hope. It was then that I was being prepared and groomed for the work and dreams I've lived out to this very day.

I started speaking in Texas Boys Town also on KNOK 107.5 FM with my mentor, Rev. Stephen E. Broden in Grand Prairie, Texas. Dr. Paul Cannings, our youth pastor, really made an impression on me. He believed in my standing before teens undergoing serious problems such as running away, drug abuse, crimes, and plain hardheadedness. Who knew this was what I would end up doing for the rest of my life? I loved being a member of Oak Cliff Bible Fellowship Church in Dallas under the leadership of Dr. Tony Evans.

A person is known by his or her consistent actions. During my rap recordings and public appearances, I share these triumphs. Have you heard the story of another Miami homeboy Les Brown? Like us, you too can be a miracle once you learn how to win. It was Les Brown who got through to me, reached me with his words during a talk on my middle school's front lawn.

Arthur McDuffie, my teacher's husband, who worked as an insurance man, was killed. Mrs. McDuffie made sure I attended the event and heard the radio jock, Mr. Brown speak.

Miami's biggest 1980's riot ignited on the heels of McDuffie's death. While riding a motorcycle, he was killed by police. Standing in the rear of the crowded tent on Westview's lawn, I witnessed powerful words that changed my life forever.

Mrs. McDuffie had my arm twisted under hers. She made sure that I heard every word. I was carrying a gun to school and skipping sixth-period classes daily to avoid fights and shooting someone. I had been influenced by my employers, La La Frenchie and Clarice regarding handling a life-threatening situation. When Les Brown said, "You are somebody because God doesn't make junk," I was floored. In fact this was the same quote that my mother placed over my bed.

By the summer of my freshmen year, I was ready to call it quits for my life. Yes, I was suicidal and the drugs didn't help. I cried out to God for help. The drugs didn't ease the agony of the hood. I had picked up some good traits during my visits to the Boys Club regarding prayer before practices, games, or after practices.

I was always put on the spot. Nobody asked whether I knew how to pray. Even then we were always trained or coached by football and baseball players, or other professional athletes. These were all the avenues and hooks that lifted me out of destroying my life at an early age. Dancing, karate school, deejaying, football, and skating were other hobbies that gave me a lasting impression. These activities motivated me to keep going and to want more out of life. After hearing Brown on top of all that was happening in my community, I prayed as I dialed my brother's number in Dallas. I needed him to get me out of that place in 1982.

I had already had close brushes with serious trouble and was motivated to get a life. Standing on the podium months later at The Texas Boys Ranch was quite different. The boys who sat before me had been apprehended, but I had not been caught yet! Most of the youth from my school or church were from stable middle-class homes. I was from Miami-Dade County. Once my mother gave her consent, the Cadillac cars and deejays drove me to the Miami International Airport to fly into Dallas alone. DJs and drug dealers from my neighborhood made me give my word in a promised oath. I was made to swear I would make something of myself. These were the men that rapper Rick Ross and others mention and boast about on their albums. These were the men whose cars I washed to make money. Ike Hicks, Bo' Dilley, Mr. Wonderful, Herman 'Scatter Hawk' Dixon, and others were on a first-name basis with those around the neighborhood. My point is that I never had to be a bad boy. I was exposed to enough drama and foolishness to last a lifetime. It was the Lord's guidance and intervention that helped me to survive the streets, see another day, and make it to my dreams. The Lord helped me to do that once I got motivated. "If you can look up, you can get up," Brown often says.

1

May My Livin' Never Be in Vain

I woke up this morning asking God what was on the schedule for today. A few minutes later, while ironing my pants, I had an epiphany. I prided myself on being a rap-activist. I had lived my dream. As a teen, I marched in Miami's streets with the best and most radical activists such as Joseph Lowery (SCLC), Les Brown, Ben Cowan, and Dr. Marvin Dunn. In 2006, my son Devon T. Sutton was killed in Miramar, Florida. He was either breaking up a fight or defending a cousin when he followed some older guy to a car and the suspect shot him in the head. After I spoke up in the media, police, hours later, found the killers. This is a story that hit the front pages of the Miami Herald and Sun-Sentinel. Anyone can Google "Teen shot, killed after fight that ended Miramar dance" ... it's real painful to write about but I do talk about my loss.

I found myself at a Dr. Martin Luther King parade marching down 62nd Street alongside former NAACP president Ben Chavis Muhammad, who was then advising rap mogul Russell Simmons. I have a rich history with being on the frontlines of a good fight as my mother had always encouraged. For a worthy cause, I was sent to prison for saving lives. I will explain further along in this journey. I was trying to stop a big gang and family war. We have too many black men going to Prison for nothing. This is one reason why I continuously requested to meet with President Barrack Obama in 2009. This is not weird or strange when you've consulted for organizations that strongly partner with the government, local civil councilmen, congress, legislatures, judges, and The White House Drug Administration. Former NFL player Rosey Grier recognizes the way in which he impacted me by simply picking up the phone in the seventies and asking for the White House operator. Grier has been instrumental in my music career as well as my professional speaking. All these details are noted in my autobiography, I'm Not a Star.

When you are from Overtown, everybody, no matter their fame or fortune, is still a human being. I remember a while back asking the Lord: "Please allow me to write all the memories of this prison incarceration." I always knew the Old Testament story of Jacob's son Joseph (Genesis 39). I too had experiences that perhaps would stop others from coming or going down the road to being a Prison Industry Product.

For some people, this is the best life they have ever had. Some never knew their parents or were raised by people who perhaps did not give a hoot about them. Three meals and a cot: institutionalized. I was always instructed by inmates doing real prison time or those who regretted being inside to reach out to kids. They always said: "Yes, you did something and got sentenced playing captain save a chick. You got caught up. But everyone who knew the situation of your case trying to stop murders and gang wars, know you don't belong here. Now you see what this is all about. Now go back and warn others keep them out of here, Mike!"

Witnessing tears welling in their eyes and streaming down their faces so often removed their hard outer-shell attitude and uncovered a heart of flesh, not stone. Those inmates had become conscious and repentant. Some rehabilitated, coming to terms with their past mistakes or actions. Most of these men either felt or saw that I was about more positivity than those holding negative reputations or braggarts about criminal careers. So it came to me that I did ask God to allow me today, not in five years, to not only go back into prisons to encourage men (my brothers) who are in a foreign territory or country. I asked Him to allow me to give firsthand accounts of how I was fortunate, to say the least, to have made it through this darkness of a hellish place that they call PRISON. I'd really like to get my point across in writing; touch the hearts of young people and caution them. I won't apologize for this intention or aim. I'd like others to benefit from someone with insight that might help reclaim their souls (mind, body, and emotions) and spirit (inner-being and image of God). Without this ability to subdue your discipline, self-esteem, or whatever your higher power might be, you are considered an animal that needs to be caged. Society does not face the reality about the people they lock up. They forget the people who Jesus mentioned as being the least among them: prisoners, the lost and the poor. Crime is big business, but GOD is still up to something great for those that can see His hand in the fire with them.

I have nothing to prove. My main prayer is that if you can reach just one person in this task it will be all the more worth it. I reflect and thoughts rush forward in my mind. There were letters written to people on the outside that are now lost. I had the strongest intent to share each detail of that part of my life. My testimony is one that I have always shared with a passion being that I was a shorty coming out of Overtown. Les Brown has declared or proclaimed often: "You all just don't know where God brought this little brother from."

During this project, I struggled a lot to focus on getting my point across to those that might pick up this writing. It is my hope that others will be given a chance to put my journey (this book) in the hands of those who will greatly benefit. I look forward to billions being impacted by this work of God in my life. Many often would tell me, "Forget the past, put all that there behind you or let it go!" It wasn't that I was stuck in the rear or stuck on stupid; I just knew that if I experienced it, it wasn't just a benefit to me. It had to have been something of a greater value that I had been given to share with others. That was just the oath taken in my community. If someone did you a favor, specifically one that you couldn't afford or have the opportunity to access on your own, they would make you swear to help or bring along someone else in return for the favor. Now these are values imparted to me missing in today's world: virtues, and rules to live by. It's the single motive in my total life mission and this book. Few fail to realize that I've already let go of the past, but not without abstracting lessons of knowledge, wisdom, and understanding. I turned 36 on September 19th, 2003. One day before my birthday, I was released from behind the fences gradually. I had been held in David L. Moss Tulsa County, Lexington Processing Center, James Crabtree (Minimum/Medium Yard), Lawton Wackenhut Correctional, Jim E. Hamilton Correctional in Hodgen, Okla., and Lawton Work Center. It's the public that continues to make you remember and pay the costs for your past or foolish mistakes, choices, and behaviors. It all comes down to this one fact: they were caught and I just got away.

Everyone has a past and no one is perfect. It doesn't take much to be sent to prison. Prison is tailor made and any warm body will do—the criminal justice machine must be continuously fed. That, I feel, is a crime in itself but they gotta eat too. I have had to fight for some sanity and peace of mind often.

I write this with the reader (you) in mind. I present stories within stories and all the details to give the full scoop. I learned this as a child listening to old folks from various cultures dubbed griots tell it like it is. May all you taste, smell, feel, and recognize never vex you but bless and liberate you. Only God himself can reconcile you with your past and only when you truly trust in Him as His creation and His child, period. It is through great appreciation for all people and my love for Christ Jesus that I made it to this day. I thank all of you from the deepest parts of my heart and soul—all those who cared for me in spite of it all, whatever it was. May my living never be in vain, as written in the famous song by Mahalia Jackson, entitled: If I Can Help Somebody.

> If I can help somebody, as I pass along,
> If I can cheer somebody, with a word or song,
> If I can show somebody, how they're travelling wrong,
> Then my living shall not be in vain.
>
> Chorus:
> My living shall not be in vain,
> Then my living shall not be in vain
> If I can help somebody, as I pass along,
> Then my living shall not be in vain.
> If I can do my duty, as a good man ought,
> If I can bring back beauty, to a world up wrought,
> If I can spread love's message, as the Master taught,
> Then my living shall not be in vain.
>
> Chorus:

2

Charged

Time stood still on April 4, 2001. It had been months since I had been in Atlanta's audience at the Stellar Music Awards getting my praise boogie on and slapping daps next to Kirk Franklin and Yolanda Adams. I always went the extra mile to support the former gang leaders of Los Angeles' The Gospel Gangstaz or other similar groups. By that time, I already had audience and private conversations with M.C. Hammer in a couple of cities. I had already told Tupac how he would die if his thug life was not really dead prior to his signing with Death Row Records. We had just had other rap artists in Tulsa and a short tour with Tupac's bodyguard Big Frank Alexander who became a Christian. One of my public school students who would often call my house to let me know how she was doing was nothing unusual for me an active young minister.

The female student I had been counseling and assisting called my house. I received this here off-the-wall telephone call just as I was about to turn in that night. I slipped on my Dallas Cowboys silk warm ups after giving 9-1-1 instructions to a young lady who wishes to remain anonymous. I am proud of her to this very day with all she has accomplished. "I am on my way!" These were the last reassuring words I can never forget. I drove on over to the house to meet police in route.

My now ex-wife the week before had decided to pack up the children. She once again left me in our empty house without explanation. After I, under close spiritual advisement, told her that she needed to get a part-time job to help out, she wanted a divorce. I was changing clothes on that day for my third sideline job: bodyguard. Supporting the family and paying child support for my son Michael was serious business. The student in trouble at home was indirectly associated and related to another client of mine. That client was a promoter who always told people, including his family, that I was his bodyguard. Often at events I had to also secure his family and relatives, something included in my job description. I was used to all types of intervention with churches, schools, juveniles, courts, judges, and DAs or civil officials who called on me from time to time.

The child whose family I worked for who was now calling because she was experiencing problems at home. The school counselors, teachers, security, and principal had originally instructed me to assist in this so-called difficult student. Few children in school ever gave me a real problem—I became their problem if they made my day. One student assigned to me would fight on the school buses, all around the campus daily and in the classroom. I made the adjustment as always when requested. Besides the safety of the principal and then staff from the visiting public, I was spread like Miracle Whip on most days. At my side and out of class this student would rant and rage. I would usually post up between the counselors office, the school entrance and the principal's office, and halls along with the lunchroom traffic in the breezeway. Eventually, I began to tune into this raging and talkative child: a little girl who was later calling and reporting in during her crises. I often would ask my wife to partner, to come alongside these females instead of me constantly being called upon. I saw in these children what my wife had said that she'd experienced growing up, and what I somewhat feared for my own daughter: signs of abuse, PTS, and defensive-combativeness against negative views of black men. I took the time to question all the things the student reported regarding what was about to happen at her home and in the community, and why she behaved the way she did in school. I thought for the most part that it was all a show, unreal. Perhaps she was simply seeking attention. Many days I got calls to sit or go sit in classes where kids were out of control, especially the African-American students. The teacher either was fed up, too geekie, or had her hands tied in the school's office with another disciplinary situation. Immediately, I could bring a class under control and do a short survey of them, their environment, and more. I'd learn why the teacher or instructor was gone and the assignment that needed completion. I was already a licensed public school educator. I was not new to the classroom leadership role. Upon gathering the facts, the office staff regularly listened over the PA system to the order and conduct of the class. I had learned a little about the students. Some lived with relatives, grandmothers, aunts, or others. When they crossed the line about my personal life I gave a general overview of my family, church, and my role at the school. These were things listed in my job description. I had to get close enough to these students to sniff out any lingering dangers and be professional as a head armed security staff member / counselor, as I was described. Teaching had always been second nature to me. The poverty was very real to these students and their active minds. Once a teacher had been robbed; someone had gone inside her purse. As the kids would say affectionately, "She got jacked, rolled on."

I often touched a chord when students wanted to know about Jesus or have a spiritual conversation. Some got so relaxed speaking or sharing about their home lives. I knew they could feel the light in me. Issues and experiences would spill from them and cause another classmate tell the truth or paint their own story. They mostly wanted everyone to know how their lives came to be what it was: mom or dad in jail, on crack, who was gang banging—it was all exposed. It was the same bits and pieces I've heard all around the country, in courts, in principals' offices, city council meetings, or in churches; in rap music. One thing that stood out so often was that they recognized and acknowledged the presence of not only an African American hip sort of male image that appeared to them as one who could relate to their issues. I was a grown man, something that represents a father figure—what many lacked in their homes.

3

Marriage on the Rocks, Please!

I returned home from my apartment in South Tulsa separated from my wife, by choice. It was done out of respect and to avoid fighting or other confrontation. I went out and got my own apartment to rethink the direction in which the marriage was headed. Her dad warned me that she was like her mom and "knew how to bring lots of drama." Stubborn was the word he used on June 1, 1998, while I was unloading the truck and moving into my first rental home in Tulsa. I always assumed her dad to be venting about something else. I wanted the marriage to work. Natasha, Joe Frazier's daughter had flown into town while I was separated for my birthday. All she was waiting for was for me to start and finish a divorce. Natasha and I could have become involved. Really. But we remain friends to this day—kind of.

During this time, I was working in the schools when the governor of California didn't grant a stay for the execution of former gang leader Tookie Williams. I wasn't moved by Lil' Kim about to go to prison or her gimmick songs about oral sex: How many licks does it take to get to the center of a tootsie roll? Tookie's situation, all the work he got into to transform lives and teach a more positive way to live, was devastating to me and others that could relate to him. Time Magazine published all the phony charges men- young black males were catching in New Orleans and around the United States. Black men were being locked up at higher rates than usual. I spent most of my weekends jumping out of a Rolls Royce and other limos. In clubs, I was asked to hop on stage and bust a rap flow with rock or jazz bands. Life was good. I was called over the PA and told that my wife and children were there in the office and asked what I wanted them to do. I was covering a class once again when I got the call. This was certainly a surprise and I told the administrator to stand by I would take care of it. I then immediately rounded up two responsible students to go to the front office and retrieve my estranged wife and my children whom I dearly loved. I instructed these students on how to best represent, the school and Mr. Mike. I was always called this affectionately and took it serious when my name was called. Respectfully, the students returned escorting my children and their mother to this classroom at the very end of the northwest hall of the main office. I write this because my wife commented: "Wow, I went to school here once. This hall is a long walk."

The year before, we had both done a school assembly at a middle school. Whatever she had going on, our marriage took a lot of turns. We had been to visit Miami and she hated it. I was working a lot and we just didn't have the right blend of personality. Although busy with the family, I was laid back. I never had a father to teach me things, so I was ill-prepared for much. I just worked at life and did my best.

4

Lord, Help Me!

I could tell that the hallway was long from the heaviness of her breath. I leaned forward from the teacher's desk and glanced to my left at my family visiting the classroom. I excused myself and gave firm instructions to the students to finish their work and behave. I took it all in as we swiftly chatted in the hallway. "I just wanted to stop by and bring you a copy of the house keys, and say hi," she had said. She had the opportunity to see what I did aside from speaking to students during the hundreds of assemblies nationwide. I always shared my heart with her and knew when she was stroking me as the polite and caring wife. I would remember why I married this light, bright sorror. When not in a panic or having mood swings, she was wonderful. I thanked her for coming, for stopping by, and had the same students escort her back to her car. This is what really got around the school: there at Monroe Middle School, I had a family. In Florida at Scott Lake Elementary, I cried.

Around 1993, after tutoring some students with homework in the Crestview Elementary area in front of the Joe Robbie / Pro Player Stadium, I sat at the light of 183rd Street and 22nd Avenue and cried out to God for help. I asked Him, "Please

Father, make me bigger than I was to be able to reach every child and solve so many of the community problems." The eighties baby crises: grandmothers and families with crack babies, students in foster care because their mothers died of AIDS. This was all heavy to the core. The church wasn't addressing any of this, I thought. Once my wife was gone to run her errands the entire school echoed, "Mr. Mike's wife and kids came to our class. Mr. Mike's got a family. We saw Mr. Mike's little kids!" My stuff was out there but in a good way by example.

Students would be so amazed of how someone that was supposedly a baller or big-timer could care enough to be amongst them. They never really believed that Mr. Mike was somebody, until the truth came out. They all felt the abandonment but not as much as me. In that Tulsa classroom the hands went straight up. The questions were many. They recognized that Mr. Mike wasn't lying. He had already spoken about himself honestly. The students around the school started saying "Mr. Mike is my daddy!"

What shocked me was the way in which the entire class took turns after all the raised hands. I was hit with loads of questions. "Mr. Mike, will you be my daddy?" They didn't know I was just moving back home to my own house where I paid the mortgage. I was heeding advice of my lifelong mentor Pastor Stephen E. Broden in Dallas, who instructed me to go get my family back and explain to my wife about my three jobs. I had left home so I would avoid having to put my hands on my wife who was oftentimes rude and disrespectful. Although she'd hit me or throw things in rage, I withstood it all, as I have in most of my relationships unbeknownst to others. Students merely knew that they saw what they needed in their own homes, lives, and families. I've seen it before too many times. They saw a void in their own communities and school settings. This use to make me cry for years in schools I began working in Miami-Dade County Schools as well as most schools I toured with Double Impact Assemblies in the United States from 1988–2009.

There was one troubled, student, a male, about whom I continued getting intervention calls from the main offices or counselors to "Please assist us!" Eventually, after supervising this be-my-daddy class, I had to escort him out of the school. He had just been expelled for allegedly carrying a gun. "He would soon be returning to do damage to the school or staff, if we weren't careful," I was told by office staff to which he repeated the message. These were issues that I had warned city council and legislators about over the years. This was happening around a lot of the community of Tulsa County. I never took this sidebar of information lightly.

Of all the public school news interviews I've done over the years, even warning Colorado officials of the exact school Columbine, few in those tall oil company buildings in downtown Denver listened to me until it was too late. The church I worked for in the city had a sponsoring Church Bowls community. I was recommended by a Promise Keepers board member to connect with Bowls. Each year I would speak to youth and do trainings in different churches. The word on the streets from these youth students was about the so-called Trench Coat Mafia. They wanted me to come to their schools and address it. By then I had already warned Tupac (1994–95) that the streets would kill him if his thug life was not over. He went on to sign with Death Row Records and was later killed. All the tears and letters from me and my students didn't help much. I know who killed Tupac, and Delores Tucker was the first source of it all. I had wised up and fell for the corporate security industry's stats to strap up and meet force with force. If it was deadly you'd have to level the playing field to save lives. All the metal detectors I installed and supervised in courthouses and now schools and this: I now carried a state licensed chrome nickel plated .357 with the black pistol grip. I tested at the top percentile in both armed and unarmed licensing in 1998 and 1999. I preferred a Bible instead until off-duty detectives showed me the reality. A man with a mental case enters the bank and a staff member sent for me to calm and remove a customer who wants his disability check from his account. Once I walked the Vietnam veteran outside, he made the wrong move. Unarmed, I was still awaiting my weapons permit. The bank staff had called into 9-1-1 as a possible bank robber. The cops walked over and stood next to me as I asked the fellow to leave. He went into his pants and both cops drew their weapons at each side of his head. I was there in the parking lot with the man looking down both barrels. This was the same rule taught during our course training. They had the drop on him and me too. Scared and speechless, I gladly obeyed when instructed to step back. The situation was calmed and diffused in seconds. The man was also known by these detectives and released.

On school grounds, running a crew of older armed fellows feeding my family with my Gideon Bible tucked in my back pocket, I escorted a young African American out the side of the west wing doors saving him embarrassment from other students. I thought, how often as a youth I was that same kid, never caught.

5

Tellin' It Like It Is:
Let Me Clear My Throat

I'm not bouncing around in my description of things or subject exactly. Stories inside of real stories are how I actually explain and present the whole story in true. This isn't how people read the Bible they just pull scriptures without considering the surrounding elements of the full history, the chapter or verse.

I'm like the old people in Miami who raised me. I want you to hear and see each piece, the whole story inside out as if you were there or it was you in the event of things. Recently, a former Florida State prisoner Sharon told me as I let her know I must get back to finishing this book you are reading now: "Give it to them raw, Mike! Somebody may need to get it just like that, okay!" No fluff, no disrespect to the grammar rules exactly. I learned to read and write differently. Studying lyrics of Michael Jackson was English class to me. Grammar has rules for a reason and can constrict the most creative, if you allow it. I leave that to the pros. Few remembered the origin of the English language and how it was conceived from so many others to make one language. Anyway, that's another story about what is considered a bastard language and who stole what. I want to be clear no doubt, no fat and to the point. Creative people tend to beat around the bush; circle the block in emotions and passion while communicating. I'm really one of those people. Show me some empathy ... but to embellish my own life story isn't necessary. My family can tell it better, that's not a miss. I gotta keep it real as an in-ci-dence, meaning to the extent or rate that it occurred. I've got bends and curves with no real apologies. I have to get it out to you the best way I know how and that's just "telling it like it is." Telling it straight like Richard Wright. You will have to backtrack like a private eye and piece it together yourself. Reporters and real writers can present conservative approaches. I leaned on the side of having to hold back so much some audiences or people are not ready for it all in one sitting. I merely attempted to put the brush in hand and paint, illustrate as best possible. Shorthand, lyrical rhymes, poems are more of my abstract thing. As far as transitioning properly, I write the way I speak, I'm told. I speak with various paint colors and pitches also pure sincerity always. I don't mention anything that hasn't already been discussed and written about me in national news, magazines, radio or television, or heard in my music. The operative phrase is "my story, my music and my life." It's been my therapy and few know this. Like LL Cool J, Todd Smith, a former client put it, "I make my own rules." In one Tulsa Middle School as the word got around to not only students, I had come to be known on a first name basis. But the teachers and other counselors would say: "Please come to my classroom, or my office, Mr. Mike!"

I'm hoping this child I just spoke with doesn't do nothing stupid as he is finally off the school property heading home to stay, we all hoped. I wanted to cry as I saw myself in that young boy, knowing that he was falling through the cracks of the system. And later, he did. On my visit to Radar Juvenile Detention-Prison in 2004, in the audience, there he was. He had become known for committing several drive-by murders in Tulsa. I close with that story, my friends.

6

Green Mile: The Movie

Eventually I had to follow up to see if his grandmother received him. I'm then called into a classroom near the door of the same west wing. I can't forget the science teacher, a short white fellow who called me to a classroom crowded with bugs and plants. Unlike before, he asked me to enter inside to watch his class for him. Here we go again, I thought. I had bigger fish to fry. I'm the one they put at the front of the school when students want to be returning gunmen. How could I sit with this class of wild children? This was a passion of mine: to save lives through education. Yet I couldn't tell the instructor where to stick his class. In fact, it was opposite to the class my ex-wife visited prior. Like the students, the teacher mentioned that he was an actor who had made a movie or was in one, The Green Mile. I thought, great! Even when I'm not in Hollywood (my annual vacation spot), everybody is a movie star. I never believed him.

I had a court appointee, Anwar Leathers, from the judges at the juvenile detention center in Tulsa County, who begged and wanted me to watch this movie. I'd fall asleep each time someone started the DVD for about a year or two even after meeting the teacher. I had rappers like Lil' Kim and bodyguards going to jail or (the legendary Tookie Williams) being killed on death row in LA, running through my mind. I had limos to jump out of for Nelly on Billboard Charts riding high in fame, Toni Estes on Priority Records, Charlie Wilson / The Gap Band and Snoop Dogg Boys locally to keep under safe wraps. I had so much like this going on and getting my family on track, especially my baby girl Destiny growing fast. It was all going on with a new rap album Eulogy looking promising with Leo Okeke, a double-platinum producer.

Joe Frasier and I finally met. His daughter learned I was separated and flew down for my birthday. "Like what, you mine now!" she had said. I had to fight the devil and save sweethearts and get my family again, I thought.

The day it hit me, I had instructed this man's class twice, I was bugging hard laughing. He really was that crazy guard guy chasing that mouse. It was teachers and staff like him that cracked me up. They recognized that I had a positive influence with students and would say, "Yo- Black man over here help me brother with your people or these children!" They didn't always have a handle on these kids. Few never looked up the definition of the word "kid." It means: a young stubborn goat or, occasionally, antelope.

7

Everybody's Daddy

The word got back to one a young lady I had been stuck with for several days. I always insisted they let her go back to class, or make her go away. They suspended the rest, why not here too? I always saw it as church work in a working man's clothing in the community. This never changed. This is how I was taught in other cities and growing up. Some would bring me their report cards, or want to leave class to tell me something. There were times that I had to report situations involving students that broke my heart, especially their behaviors. That's middle and high school for you. Now I was everybody's daddy, right?

I could only give so much attention to the students at one time. Some days I couldn't go to lunch in peace. I really didn't mind the interruptions. All the kitchen and school staff knew "they need to let Mr. Mike eat his lunch." If I wasn't hiding, my tray of food was always prepared, wrapped, and set aside for me most days.

One day I had to push my plate away because security and other staff were insisting that I go to a school counselor's office at the southwest wing, "right away." They were blowing up my radio. I was eating this good plate of food and had turned that radio off. After a long night shift post of work, I needed that food badly. One student assigned to me by staff often was acting out again: running around the room, making threats, rants, and just in crises.

"Call my momma, call the police. Put me in jail. I'm going to ..." she lamented. Once I arrived keeping my weapon intact and entered the room, staff said, "This child says you are her daddy." I knew the running jokes and rumors had taken a serious turn. I saved face and sat down, thinking as I took my seat. Without all the details, I look this student in the face and went off. "Look, you know better than this." I named the counselor who stuck her with me.

It turned out with her being so smart that she picked up the rumors and didn't want her family or parents to get involved with what she was going through at school. I paused again, with staff and asked to let me have a few words with her. This was almost an everyday thing with students, but not like this. Eventually, we got to the bottom of it all. I was assigned to keep her with me all day for a while. She kept mentioning she knew me and all. She mentioned that she and her family knew me. I had been at work on so much and involved in so many incidents, situations and media frenzies. I usually ignore the rapper, the popularity and the "you somebody important" stuff. These were my platforms. Her argument was: "No Mister Mike, you work for my family! You work for us and I can prove it. Remember ..." I was surprised about what she knew of my private clients: Trick Daddy, Trina, Sole, LeVert, Bones & Thugs, and others.

I moonlighted as a third or fourth job to secure and escort

people with a limo company, if the money was right and in cash. I had gotten back into this seriously thanks in part to Tupac's main bodyguard Big Frank Alexander. We'd become close and I felt how serious he took his job in escorting me. We toured Oklahoma and we (the Ministry) wanted to encourage him after Tupac's death. I attempted to mentor Tupac spiritually during his incarceration in Clinton MAX. Big Frank filled in a lot of Death Row pieces of Pac's last days for me. Frank gave me so much inspiration. I was hard on Tupac and rejected his new albums until he died—as I told him he would. I was sad even though reporters and others wanted me in the news talking about all the positivity I bought his way. My protective service advanced to an entirely different level since I returned to the schools and was carrying a gun. When Tupac died I had four guns, especially after Columbine and all the other deaths around me. My buddy Victor Nellum's sister and students I worked with at East High School had been shot gang-execution style. Vic's sister was the only one who lived. Denver was a dark city during this time. I was fed up.

Now up and close with the student, I had to backtrack with her on it all and she had been saying her family this and that. She spoke of all the past, current, and future problems that was about to go down. So many tried to twist the plot of how I got involved in this domestic matter that I was about to dive into by interpretation. It was because I worked off-duty for the family that she knew me, and now I'm her daddy too. It made it no better when her grandfather, a churchgoing elder with an interesting past, came to the school. I was told to meet him in the school office. We sat and talked as I listened.

He confirmed everything the child had been saying, screaming, and pounding down our throats. No one was really listening. C-Y-A is always the public policy to protect you and your job or family. After the introduction to the other side of the family of this child's kin, I swiftly met with the school principal. She was a straight up trip and disgrace in fancy clothes and a Christian sister too. She was politicking for the school board's agenda like in the movie Lean on Me. What I am saying is that if you don't know the game, you become the pawn in the game. The grandfather confirmed everything was all true. He said to her, "Why don't you all listen when a child is trying to tell you something?" He had already told me what the deal was already. He put his gun to his son-in-law's head (her dad's face) and said, "If you put your hands on my daughter again, I'm gonna kill you!!!" Whoa, this was the impending doom the child was raging about—a family war of wars. To make matters worse, other distant relatives were curious for more than thirteen years about this domestic abuse of their relative. They knew it all from the other men in the family far too long. The little girl's father had been despised at family gatherings for years. The family's in-laws and out-laws wanted to rope him up and rope him off. Where would intervention best be served now? Somebody was really about to get their cap peeled or pushed back; become cornfield fertilizer from deep down under. Serious, you gotta see how country people think. Real city-life violence is only an urban version. Didn't you see how the real Bumpy Johnson or American Gangster and others ruled in New York through country boys off the farm?

My wife joined me to rally up the at-risk students that received their parent's permission for a special meet and greet with some celebrity clients of mine with whom I was touring that had new albums released. Surely it was no problem. The uncle was the area promoter of all the artists. Since I had spoken at this same school before a year prior to me working there and their other principal retired. I saw that sharing the after fellowship portion was on time with these students. The same would be after an actual concert of mine, to eat, talk, and laugh out loud, or, food, fun and fellowship is how we put it. Like then it's just normal for me to break bread and give up close encounters to break the ice and star / fame junk with people. It's a platform for the mass message not the lifestyle. The two are separate.

Returning home for me was perfect so the wife could give her shared reflections also being a former student of that school or the school system in which her mother worked. While the pizza and other foods were being served, I worked my way around the room of Mazzio's on Pine and Harvard. I met some parents there who sat nearby. Upon one polite introduction by his sons, I felt this man's distance. Chris Lewis was thick. He was standoff-ish and laid back. After thanking him for allowing his child to take part in the off-campus after-school activity, I began to discuss how I came in contact with his troublesome daughter. It was not my business, but it was part of the intervention I performed. I mentioned the grandfather's visit to the school after one of her many outbursts concerning the family rivalry. He gave more of his attention to how I told him that "domestic violence really does affect children in the homes and especially little girls becoming women." As I pointed at my wife, who was engaged with the students, I gave an overview of her past family experiences and my own. "My father was shot by my mother seven times and he almost died. I was a baby." The girl's father somewhat relaxed and I later departed from the table. I returned to the crowd and greeted other coworkers having a family night out. We all had a good evening, especially with my own children being given all of the attention from the students there. We even ended in prayer as my other coworker's families joined in.

7

Okay, Who Is Mr. Mike?

Eventually I had no real idea that my student would be questioned by her biological father the following week often about "Who is Mr. Mike? Okay, who is Mr. Mike? How does he know the family's business?"

Weeks later after the Tom Joyner air show left Tulsa, one of my newest clients had a gig in town to do the Black Expo event. By this time, I grabbed a partner of mine to work the crowd with me. Eric was getting a chance to kick it with me in action some on the bodyguard side of things for once. It became clearer to all parties in how we all knew each other and that I was working for all of them at events of intense drama, rap concerts and in limos. I was unfamiliar with all of my client's extended relatives, but that is how it is in the country too. They all knew my steps with the singer. I got a call in route from a student insisting that she's "gotta come and see this singer" while I meet her mother. We were exiting the venue rushing to the exit door with my trainee assist next to me. They were here and we were stopping autograph seeking fans who wanted more of Toni Estes' time. We said our hellos, shook hands, and went the opposite direction. Upon my client's acknowledging she was ready to go, the child's mother announced: "That's our family bodyguard!"

9

Nobody Listening

Weeks later I was debriefed on the brewing gang war that would spark off if domestic violence went down in this state. I had already had a face-to-face with the city mayor, Susan Savage. I had already on multiple occasions gone to the city councilmen for whom I'd worked security three-and-one-half years. I told them even before meeting these new people that this is the word on the streets. Street news is real news before it happens and afterwards on the right streets. The onslaught of dead bodies from gang turf wars was real and unsolved to this day.

Bodyguards to the Stars

I was already use to being in hotels, hotel rooms, backstage, in clubs, restrooms, limos, closed rooms and in alleys where deals were cut and someone could be bleeding coming in or going out. Public schools really are a playground in this field sometimes. I was use to the confidentiality penalty of life or death. I was always the listening and look-away gun since I was a baby. Trust what I'm saying on this one. When a client starts talking about killing, killing cops and that Godfather I,

II, III, and IV stuff. People don't know it's real. I've been known to have to check that and declare: "I'm a Christian man! I ain't doing that and I ain't killing no cops or no body for that matter." When promoters, property owners, and politicians feel a pinch from authorities or that they are being shook down, they become vengeful.

I always have heard the most dangerous call for a police officer is a domestic violence and family feuding. It's true! God bless the dead. My Miami Central Senior High School alumni and classmate, Carey, died behind that (breaking it up stuff). One day in 1993, he was thanking me for changing my life from the Luke / 2Live running days to visiting prisons and schools telling me how proud of me he was and what he read and heard in the news. The next day, I was getting ready for the Bahamas and my album release party cruise on international waters when my brother died. "He was going over to his neighbor's to break up a fist fight, stopping a guy from beating his wife and the husband or someone killed him," the news reported.

When I returned home a week later, I had the opportunity to speak at my former elementary students' middle school, Parkway. I had to tell this sad story. Funny, the class I was speaking in was that of my 1985 class president, Keith Harrell, who is now a school principal. Keith lost his brother Kevin a similar way: murder. The good part was that my childhood friends knew of my work around the world in Los Angeles, Texas, Ohio, and Michigan. Carey stopped me on 111th Street and 17th Avenue and said to me, "Mike, in school I never liked you and I always just wanted to kill you every time I saw you so bad and I don't know why. Now I see all the good you are doing for people and I'm glad for you. Keep doing what you are doing." I was shocked as my mouth dropped wide open as I waited for my auto to be repaired in the corner shop. I thanked him too and I remembered seeing him in school just as he had described.

The next day, he tried to do some good in the hood and now he's gone. These things happen every day and I wish I could help stop it somehow. It's been my mission since as a child I witnessed a man gunned down in the rain in Overtown. Blood everywhere, from a machine gun. I was trapped between my mom and the babysitter's house when he was blasted and his body was jolted to the impact of the bullets, likely twenty to forty rounds. This is one reason I never liked guns. It is another reason why recapping and expressing this journey can be so difficult.

Wearing Many Hats

Meanwhile, I get the full details on what is going to affect the community as a whole. Nobody said that there were police officers one both sides of the family. In hindsight, the plot was so thick I knew that if anything my intervention was all figured out meaning STOP THE KILLINGS, period! This is my motto from childhood and it was no simple way of looking at it. Had I seen or met these officers before? I didn't know! Were they there when the Sheriff banded Nelly's limos and his appearances and I was called to explain the effects and consequences to the law enforcement and owners of the Big Splash facilities?

Country Grammar had hit the number one spot on Billboard Music Charts as I was being assigned to the artist of the same name: Nelly & The St. Lunatics. It was only the Lunatics that basically performed outdoors so professionally. Between venues, we'd all forgotten to eat. Everything moving so fast and they were vegetarians but not me. I needed real food. Both Nelly's and my stomach ached from not eating. We were so busy in crowds and all the whole nine. People don't know what real stars, fame, and appearances do to you. The sacrifices really have to be made. At this time, I was wearing many hats, to say the least: the wife, children, bills, property upkeep, and three jobs (corrections, security, and body-guarding). It felt like five with my own company and helping to run someone else's business, not to mention the various sites. Forget my own recording and speaking career dates. Much began to lack as I met those child support payments in Florida for lil' Mike the best way I could and still feed the family at home.

10

Taking Our Child

I missed one concert date: April 2001. That's when it all went down. I was supposed to be headed to Texas with Evangelist Big Jon for a Youth Concert event. By this time my wife was telling me that she was taking the kids to "where I couldn't see them anymore. Across state-lines," she said matter-of-factly. She stated that she wanted a divorce after I explained to her that she needed to take on at least a part-time job. I was shocked. I felt my heart drop as I rushed into the bathroom to change gear for my other job assignment. I offered her money on the spot to feed my children.

The next day she had taken the kids and was gone in the wind. I won't lie. I was dumbfounded, cuckoo, loco, vido. I called the lawyer. I called longtime pastor friends nationwide to pray with me. I couldn't shake it—my family was gone. The house was quiet. My daughter wasn't running up to the door when I came home or wrapping her tiny arms around my legs as I entered the house. I called my then-hommie Eric. "EL, this is what it is. Let's go shopping. Dinner's on me, dawg." I shopped til I dropped and still couldn't shake it. Why this here woman gonna go do this and I'm doing everything I can to please her and her parents?

I had uniform gear but never had enough current casual like street clothes on my assignments. I had to dress for the job and when you are on the town with your clients whether they are celebrities, ministries, or government officials, you must dress the part. I can hear you saying: "This book is about him bodyguarding!" It's not. It's about how my ministry work began as G.A.S. (Gangs, Addicts, and Stars), the people I reached out to daily through my different roles and what happen to me in general.

11

Gospel Music Stellar Awards

The small cameo during the Stellar Awards in Atlanta's Arena Theater in 2001 was not a bad way to start the New Year. I never cared for those types of festivities, but I'm glad I did get to become a part of that history in Gospel Music with 50 million television household viewers and all that took place there only by the grace and hand of God. I didn't know supporting award nominees 2G'z-Gospel Gangstaz, former Crips and Bloods from Los Angeles, all of whom I've supported for over fifteen years would be so enjoyable. I was ministering all the way there on the road with an ole 2 Live Crew and then MC Hammer's Bustin Records manager Darrell Butler in Mississippi. God Bless the souls of the deceased.

Not even my wife would support this trip, at least not at first. She had to pray a lot and hear God after I had to iron and press my own gear and pack myself as usual, and jumped into the rental zee box and then jetted. I always called my wife and family before I hit any county line. This was the real life I was into daily as a Miami boy doing big thangs and then later in ministry after I flipped the game. When you can drive from Miami to New York or Miami to Los Angeles with no sleep, you's a bad boy. It was about going where the light of Christ wasn't and being a light in darkness. It wasn't dropping dope or moving it around. As I told Tupac: Once you out the game sometimes going back, it could kill you ... take your life!

12

Get Involved

Letting God use you amongst those living on the edge is really what this book is about. I read everybody else's books. Afterwards, I wrote most of them and told them what they left out and broke it all down for them, if it was what went on in Miami. I told LL and Bobby Brown all the stuff they were saying about how tough and real our cities were to them. Some even wanted to rob them when I became their security. Like Luther Campbell, I'm from where Trick Daddy said it best, "we from the homes where gangsters roam all night long and they love the kids." Most times for ministers it's their time to speak when all has really been said and done. God will take all of that and roll it up and then have the man of God spit it back and break it all down in one shot, across the board. I was called not just as a pioneer of and in hip-hop music, God made me a minister to the rap and hip-hop generations at the appointed time and that's what you are embracing as the journey continues of a modern day Joseph story. Everybody in my hometown and others who know me in the music business knows this about me. My former pastors who had churches filled with celebrities, players from the NFL and NBA, know exactly who I am called to reach. I am just modeling the lifestyle shown me for the positive. This is how I grew up before I made it into the church, I grew up amongst celebrities. On my way into the church, I saw other friends dying and I was on the run from the big boys with big letters behind their names. I didn't know it, but I could always sense trouble or smell death coming. I hate it, friend. Coming from Miami, I knew each side of the tracks. My mother said that she'd "show me both sides of the tracks and fence." I would have to one day choose the side on which I wanted to live. You can see how this book and my life work came to be so real. I'm hoping others will choose the right side of the tracks that leads to life and not death. I come from a family of gangsters, musicians, religious leaders, and educators. I never had an interest in a church and I never wanted to step foot into one until the age of 15 or 16. I never saw a church leader like my mother, who was a nurse and in the streets. She helped people all the time. Sometimes she'd just sit and cry. No matter the good she'd do, sooner or later someone was doing her wrong. It never mattered who you were, what you had done, or how you did it my mother would reach out to help. She only attended church with me once or twice in my lifetime. This is all I know: Get it for yourself and give it back to the people. This must've been why Momma was trying to save that man's life when I was little.

Behind Miss Libby's store, my momma screamed and shouted, "Get help, get help!!!!" I looked down from upstairs at the man lying under the stairs bleeding and watched him convulse. That nurse's aide student, my momma, wasn't getting him off the ground. Life wasn't the same since that day for me. When Momma talked about God or Jesus I listened because it was rare. Instead, she'd put it into action. You get involved if you see a good fight or cause! were her exact words. I live by them today. Do you have some words or decrees you live by? I believe that I have the faith my mother modeled for me once she saw how I changed.

I told you, I've been around stuff all my life. It's the church that balances the crime, distortions and SIN of our abandoned communities. Poverty is a sin and people are losing their minds there or trying to get out. No government is going to end poverty. Only GOD can if the people chose to empower themselves. Few understand the messages of Reverend Dr. Martin Luther, Jr. or Michael Jackson's music. These two spread Jesus' message: get involved. "Be the change you want to see in the universe. Get involved."

Below is the letter my mother Maerene C. Newton-Pennington a.k.a. "Mrs. Joey" wrote to me in the U.S. Army about my temper.

> 1481 N.W. 103rd St, #356, Miami, Fla. 33150
> May 30, 1986
>
> Hi my big son no.4,
>
> I got your card & I was glad to hear from you-your commander letter & yours came together- I really miss you-what are you doing in S.C.? I thought you were still in Florida, just for 6 weeks. Basic Training not all the way in S.C.- a long way from home- but you are use to traveling- and I am glad you like the army- you may have found your knack(your thing). I'm so proud of you, but of course, I have always been proud of all of my kids- even if at times I don't show it- you all know me- I'm not the quiet-homebody mother. But, I'm the tiger who protects the cubs. I go into a fix & rage about my kids- either I think

or feel they are being mistreated or misused- I do not hug & kiss on you all like I use to, because of your ages & your ways- but when the chips are down I'm always there if I can. I tell people my kids can only make me angry at them a few ways- that is to lie-steal and not study and get an education- and to be ill-mannered or wise- I don't really worry about them getting into problems- For the temper you-Toni and Gino carry- I inherited from my mom and it took me years to be able to try to talk to you all & try to reason about getting mad. I use to be a terror & unable to think right or wrong or even care, If I was mad- so remember- to CONTROL YOUR TEMPER- reason with yourself if the ACT you are going to do is ---bad or good for Michael's future- learn to keep people at a arm's length where they cannot get you mad enough to get in trouble- okay? We are fine- I am paying the FLP off slowly- we made a deal- I pay $200.00 a month on old bill- and keep the regular one up to date- (smile). Butch wrote me about his commission (1st Lieutenant.) okay- now- Toni told me you call her- Jonnette is moving in (MAY) okay? When I don't know- her birthday May 30- (35 yrs old) boy! I getting old- mine is June 6- I'll be 52- Sneaky is fine & says he'll write & he remembers your code signal- Julia is okay too. (crazy as ever). I know you worry about me & if I will take care of them right- but you can ease your mind- I'm all right - I love you & miss you-- be good & good luck in all you do or try to do.

Write soon-
Your Mom loves you----always MOM.

Anyone can say what they want about my mother and her past. All I know is that she was my Sister Souljah, my Angela Davis, my Josephine Baker, and a few others including Jada

Pinkett Smith. Forget these so called honorary degrees I'm said to have from others. I want a degree for the courses I find that show you how to get involved in saving lives. When I do find it, the one for me, I'll have a PhD. I needed a true degree to halt the 2001 situations I am about to unfold.

13

Bout It, Bout It

For years my track record spoke for itself. What people do is who they are or appear to be. I've always been about the Lord once I became enlightened. I have and will make mistakes. Once discharged from the army, I was running around with rap groups like 2Live Crew with my cousin who was actually like a very big brother like mentor especially in football. Melvin Bratton got me off of the FMC campus where I was about to be ganged up on by a high school alumni and a dude I went to school with. Who could this one guy be? He attended the Alternative/Opportunity School next door to our high school. It's actually the place I would've ended up in if I didn't take that tenth-grade detour to Texas. When trouble found me, I made it a good dance partner. Another of my relatives and a former classmate found out I was home from the army and away at an Opa-locka school and rounded up some muscles. The UM Players got out of their cars four-to-six deep and were ready to rumble as Melvin approached the fellow face-to-face. These turned out to be most of the guys from my middle and high school days of football and hommies. For the most part it was like this all my life as a youth. If I was out and about and someone had it in for me, someone who knew me better stepped in, ready to open a can of whip-a**. I was blessed this way because one, my family was known in the community in certain circles. Two, anyone who knew me knew I could take a tiny fight up a few more notches so I'd never have to look over my shoulders. In my Liberty City environment, like in Overtown, people took you out. Forget a toe-to-toe fight. I had my karate training and more from the Northwest Boys Club: Shon Ryu. I was trained in avoiding problems for the time I attended the classes in between football before the neighborhood changed and it did. All of my elementary and middle school city partners were now in the suburbs of North Miami with a mix of all kinds of harder brothers. Now they've shown up at our school to save me from being a murder case, or something. My other campus buddy from Northwestern High School was just about to have a record deal with a top chart song called COLD SWEAT. I'm invited to these college events that use to be major deals in Miami with FAMU 100 marching band. That was called the Classic Parade, at which time Seventh Avenue was blocked off and everybody came out to watch the festive activities. I was living on campus and kicking it with my cousin headed to the pros (Denver Broncos). For all my old dance and rapping partners, I eventually worked as a body guard.

I had a reputation for the ways in which I handled myself in karate, boxing, and football, and Silver Blue Crash Crew Dance Group, which I found. Gary Moore and his family (a Bruce Lee fighting family) from New York helped raised me for years. Some of their nephews are members of the DMX Rough Ryders Crew, I understand. Melvin enjoins me with Luke in saying, "This is your family from now on." That night, I was immediately given Public Enemy's Flavor Flav to escort.

Some say it was a bad company of people. I say it was the family God gave me at the time fresh out the army.

I was performing X-rated rap long before I was caught by the coach on the field singing in the dark at football practice. They gave me a nickname few will never forget: Oscar Myer. This is where I came from before street deejay-ing in middle school, radio deejay-ing in high school, the college, and the army. I was officially made in Dade County. Just check my birth certificate, could a street kid save society from the same violence which he was trying to save himself?

After going from 2 Live to Christ with people dying all around me in the late eighties, I had an incident in which a producer had stolen equipment and a song he released. I was upset. AJ and some others handled it, but I was no punk and was beyond ready to settle the score with what was in my trunk. But Jordace, JDC on Luke Skyywalker Records, stopped me real fast. I will never forget the hurt and betrayal. A deep dark demon came over me: my temper. The person (Beat Master Clay D) became an even bigger music avant-garde of hip hop beats and he knew I was not playing around. I went back to church and was rejected there, but I didn't give up immediately and it paid off. My son was born, my mother had died, and feeling I'd be misunderstood all over again, I was avoiding a new record deal.

Record company executives, studio producers, bands, promoters, and other people started calling and requesting that I come pray with them or an artist of their choosing. Ice Cube, SNAP or Hammer also H-Town. Before many hit the stages or signed a record deal, they would find some way to get in contact with me. I was given this clout and more by God Himself. I never had to pose as a star. Anybody who knew me in school knew that I danced hard pop locking and rapped hard also was on the radio (WEDR) on the weekends. This was home to all the earlier giants in Miami music scene under Jerry Rushin's, our big poppa, leadership.

Though it is not as popularly mentioned, many of us, including Eric Griffin, Willie Davis aka in 3D, Pretty Tony Butler, Luther "Luke Skywalker" Campbell, and I, The PMAN aka MC DEVINE / Mike Devine came out of this radio family. This was the jump off before Dallas was for me (1981–84).

I returned to Miami to graduate in 1985, went back to Texas for college at Jarvis, and then came right back after a stint in the Army to Miami in 1986. All that back and forth kept me alive. All this led to visiting jails for exclusive prisoners, celebrities on lock down and going like backstage always with Jam Master Jay- Jason Mizell (now deceased) or with Run DMC, also at Arsenio's show in Los Angeles. When I finally did get the chance to visit churches, schools, and legislative hearings, this is what was reported around to others about what I had been doing for years even before I was engrafted to Luke's outfit, my ghetto-style family. The Florida governor's wife, Mrs. Adelle Graham, heard me and sent her support in an official letter to my dorm at Florida Memorial University. It was back then the hommies were calling it that New Jack City era and I was halfheartedly ready to get paid. I wanted to improve communities and lives away from violence and drugs. Sounded ideal, but it wasn't what was happening. In fact, I was discouraged from that type of interaction. I didn't need their money to make a difference. I needed the leaders to get involved! Back then I was a follower.

After trying to get a life and be productive, I was still a hardheaded young person with a poor foundation of discipline.

I didn't give up on me even when others did. I was grateful that others came to save my life just in time so often. This is how GAS started after I was asking Professor Griff, minister of information with Public Enemy to go get one of my former clients. His road dog, Flavor Flav, had serious trouble on Long Island. I was such a fan of these guys. Grif signed off on his record deal as Flavor had on Luke's label which had blessed me so much. It helped me to heal from so much at the time including the racial experiences from the army. I was with LL's people (George Ronnie Lyons) from Farmers Boulevard to meet up with LL and share Christ. When I returned to Miami, Grif and I were at the 127 Street U-Haul, chopping it up. This is the living on the edge ministry behind the scenes that I do. "Griff," I said. "Get your boy, man! I know you all are going through with a lot of mess at Def Jam. This is what your boy Flava up there doing and what is gonna happen to him." A week later it all hit the news. I'm just about it, 'bout it. Someone, no a few others, did it for me and I've been returning the favor every since.

April 1 and the wife and kids are still gone. I've paid off the house, had her repossessed auto returned from Texas, and gave up my leased apartment for this? I was alone in the house she grew up in for 28 plus years and still gotta go on with life. I thought, let the party begin. "Don't do anything but wait," the lawyer said. We had come to Tulsa from Denver to get involved with ministry in her former community. I guess I wasn't keeping it real enough.

I remembered the night on the town when we made up. I was on stage with another client of mine's daughter working as her bodyguard. She co-owned the VIP limo company. I was asked once more to do a freestyle rap flow to a Top 40's song. My ex-wife saw how the females, some were white, got all over me including a Russian man who insisted he wanted to dance with me for his first time in America. Crowds mounted over my table afterward as I assured the man, "I don't dance with men." My now ex-wife then told the ladies, "Back off my husband!"

This wasn't the first time she'd do such things. I just always gave the wife her first lady rights. I was taking care of home first, I believe. At the end of another day, I was turning into bed after fighting demons of an empty household. Not being able to tuck my children into their beds each night was another chalk up in gut wrenching pain.

14

2001

As I closed my eyes for prayer the phone rang. "Mr. Mike, Mr. Mike, Mr. Mike, my daddy is trying to kill my momma. I ran next door. He is choking her. He said if I call the police he'll kill her!" I always had somebody's child calling me around this time, but not like this. "Call 911 and I'm on my way!" I said calmly. The words came out and then it hit me. I jumped up and put on my shoes still in my pajamas. Someone else's child or family needed me and I was vulnerable to it all. As I drove, you could hear the fire truck sirens, helicopters, and more police. I passed the block of police and went on to meet my assistant and partner Eric (EL). "EL, what's up? I'm outside. Come on, man!" Pulling into his yard, I observed police and helicopter lights panning the full area west of the block (we were on Boston). I knew that the dad had run in our direction earlier somehow. Door-to-door searches at the girl's grandparents' home turned up empty. Down the street, we proceeded to see who the cops were keeping calm at the little girl's house. It was the grandfather I met at the school. He was standing over the girl's mother, his daughter who was now sitting on the steps being treated by paramedics as they braced her neck and then wrapped her arm in a sling. Police requested that I help the clients The Johnson family get to a safe place until the fleeing suspect, the father, was apprehended.

Mr. Johnson I watched the grandfather. After the officer commented, then Mr. Johnson stated that he wants them all brought around the corner to his house which is the backside of the home where we stood during the incident. I later realized this is where the student, prior to calling me, had run. Police allowed a few minutes more for each child (there were three to four) to gather their belongings for possibly days away from home. They packed it all in my car as I linked instructions with the grandfather and police.

The radio was bumping so I dialed up CFOX on the air. I told him about the drama that was going to keep me up for hours to come. It was straight out of a movie. He gave me and the Johnson family an on-air shout-out on 105 Fresh Jams. I tried to sleep, but couldn't as the movie In Too Deep played in the background. I went through two shifts: 9-5 then into 7 am with no sleep. Witnessing the client retrieve an emergency protective order and receive medical treatment with X-rays while performing bank site assignments was taking a toll on my mind and body. When a human life is endangered, "be prepared to shoot" is what FBI and plainclothes detectives taught me.

I had not been at this armed post long, but knew lots of people who wanted to rob that bank like crazy. This kept me a high profile person in that business district of North Point, I wasn't crazy about that fact or a few others, either. I approached this total job description with a white-gloves-on mentality. As the utility companies would receive bomb threats and threats of bodily harm to staff, you stay on your toes. This became my lifestyle as well as at the other bank locations, one where I nearly slept in the vault on 3rd and Boston literally, if not over the lobby entrance. Corporate BOA executives and the FBI wanted to see if we were on our chops at all times. It can be intense, needing to move your bowels; crapping right on the spot. From these days, I knew you stuck like Chuck without your weapon (armed and packing legally). Here I was, half sleep or half awake on the job and this happened often but nothing like what was around the corner.

The singer's dad, Billy, called. He needed me to escort her to the mall and a few clubs later that day. She had got into a fight with a lady in corrections about an ex-boyfriend. "We may need to get a protective order," I was told. Although, I was use to it, I could say nothing but "okay."

My side money picked up since the wife and kids left, yet the situation was taxing. It wasn't me in trouble—it was keeping others out of trouble that appeared to be the circumstances. Big Jon had me booked to appear in Texas and didn't know I forgot. I just wanted to sleep it all off when I've done any other overtime. I found a book in the den of our office in the desk where my wife had been writing in it about her past alleged domestic violence reports in her first marriage to Gerald McMurray. Half sleep, I had been studying the details at my job as I directed these clients the same way my boss had directed the wife in the past with her issues while he was head of their Williams Companies Security department or management. Immediately, I gave the battered client the steps to follow. I even informed the fleeing wanted ex-husband's employer, with a call asking for their assist to defuse the situation. Into the next day, the student would call in a panic. Her mom began to call often as the police patrolled the neighborhood. We had more trouble coming and it was from none of the parties present. This was becoming a stranger mix of events and still patchy with a crunch for time as the earlier child reported in school. Something got the volatility going much higher. The fleeing subject was now really in for some danger. His employer's of personnel assured me by phone at my job site that they would talk to him and warn him of impending danger that had been now aggravating. The trouble ensuing, what the student at school and the counselor gave me was the warnings about, was a war.

15

North Point

I reviewed both clients' protective orders and obtain copies in the bank lobby thanks to Mr. Busby, one of its managers, who happened to be a relative of a top police official of the district North Tulsa Police Department, Captain Busby. The report to me and police was that the dad had been leaving threatening messages on the answering machine stating that he was going to murder them. It continuously appeared to be getting intense. I left my daytime civilian post on a lunch break to see about them and check on the house property. Upon arrival, the dad was there and was abruptly leaving with his brother in white truck that was trailing his blue one. Hours prior to this time his employer's had to have contacted him. He was hurrying his things and himself out the house as I was beginning to approach from a distance. I rode up slowly. I finally attempted to speak with him about the call to his employer's office and the other call that was made to me then another call made after the 9-1-1 call the night before. It was after transporting his family that I learned all of this. The student calmly informed me of what she had done at the end of the night. She had called me, then 9-1-1, and then her out-of-town relatives who were true gangsters. These were men known to be notorious and sliding in and out of town on their way to deal with the domestic situations brewing for more than thirteen plus years. I stopped to forewarn the dad and get some insight as to who these assailants were since the dad as I was told knew them as well.

My goal was to keep all parties apart as I had informed the police the day before April 2, 2001. Thinking this was the correct intervention until police could sort it out was huge. I felt that I could ask the dad to tone it down or stop the threatening phone calls. My mistake. With all these thoughts going through my head it all happened suddenly. As I approached the father, he stopped his truck and got out as I passed. He then pulled out a shotgun. There was no talking. By the time I drew my shoulder strap weapon from beneath my plainclothes jacket and fired into the air, he was booking into his truck and down the road like hot Skippy. It was on and cracking. I was almost buckshot from behind in my automobile. He must've been afraid already of these other relatives or maybe the cops. I thought my shot in the air would scare him and he wouldn't fire on me. Once I saw him stop and get out and come out of his rear door with a weapon, all I thought was I am dead. I fired and he took off. I followed to track him only while dialing 9-1-1. I noticed my cellular phone battery was dead and attempting to plug it into the automobile lighter, I dropped it on the floor. As I approached a dead-end road's entrance, I felt bullets flying past me and shots were hitting near my car. I stopped with a half donut spin. As I looked down the road I could see we'd be in a shootout, if not a standoff. I went back to work. What I didn't know was that someone was inside of his truck who he instructed to dial 9-1-1 and report me as the wanted man. The tables had been turned. I had become the main bad guy. My boss called me later with crazy statements and I denied it all. His warrants were being suppressed as in previously reported domestic matters. I sat at home in silence and prayed while cutting my lawn and washing my car. My boss didn't have all the right pieces of information and I just wasn't about to involve him to my own fault. He checked for any outstanding warrants and police bulletins. My sideline work he always warned me of had become a big problem and now it was offsite. Maybe, if I hadn't blown him off his police contacts could've saved me the trouble and further headaches.

The next day I wasn't in Texas to perform and make an appearance. I went to work as if nothing had happened. I was then approached at my business center workstation by a huge fellow. He had questions about the events of the shooting. I saw him approaching and monitored his entrance and exit of the facilities. We had words during which time I explained "yes" your brother did this and I did that and I will protect my clients as my job goes. Both our words were short. He was gathering information and more. Upon his exit, the police tailed him. I saw his brother standing near a dollar store pay phone making a call.

As soon as he left, police came inside. I surrendered my weapon as we discussed other things. I gave my property keys to the near pharmacy tenant staff, a good associate with instructions to call my boss. This sergeant took me in for questioning seeing that I did have a license for my weapon and worked in this capacity of armed security. He had concern of the description of everything reported plus the type of weapon I was carrying. It didn't match any of the alleged reports. The sergeant who got me into the station was a kind fellow and he felt uncomfortable with the detective to whom I was presented. After I presented the client's protective order and agreed to cooperate. The detective was looking for ways to angle his questions only stopping at the description of my cars. I had not discussed anything else at the time. I saw who sat opposite his desk: a relative of the father who had just had me arrested. I saw the desk name plates in homicide often. Once the police sergeant grilled the detective with questions about it all, the detective ran and shot out of the room for more details to the matter. This was the whole behavior with all of this legal matter each step of the way. Something new popped up and they'd scramble to tie it all down fast. I got right down on the floor, handcuffed by one arm and prayed.

I was observant to pray about what I saw with these detectives and the original subject's cousin's desk, knowing by now he came from a big family. The night of the police search it was mentioned how others on the force covered this guy. I produced my weapon license for a .357. I reviewed again the emergency protective order of my client and that this man was wanted en route to harm my client as reported. The officer who brought me in was getting upset with this detective or detectives upon this one's return. The description of things didn't match even my weapon a revolver not an automatic. I was still booked as the uniformed officer whispered what I needed to do legally. He smelled a foul rat too. He was pissed off and told me don't answer anymore of the questions. Once the news spread, everyone was looking for me. Under what name had I been booked? What the city councilmen didn't say was that one of his coworkers was helping the big brother of the person involved in the incident. I knew who he was behind the scenes. His sister was my next door neighbor, and their relative was a victim of a random murder in the music circles. As a former correctional officer (a month prior to all this) and the nature of the people and their relatives involved, no one was going to find me in segregation. The warden who knew me observed all inquiries as well as his staff, my ole' buddies who knew my work in the community so strongly toward intervention and prevention. They were close associates who assisted with Tupac's bodyguard visitation into schools and other public places. They made sure I was safe even if my other client in the boyfriend dispute had her opponent or foe working in this same correctional facility. It's a small world. I was kept safe at the time, but if they want you they will try to get you in these small towns. The top jail officials and I met often, for they were saddened about these turn of events. I also worked for juvenile judges taking children into custody with threats from their families or outsiders for assisting the child and the courts. I had three to four real jobs. I wasn't just in some other people's business with all of this. I was protecting a child who committed a crime unbeknownst to even me at the time.

Jail staff visited me because I refused to eat food and fasted and prayed daily. The promoter in Texas was the only one except the limo company owner who could reach and find me locked up. The promoter Big Jon received a call through to a chaplain or doctor who then found me. It sure did feel good to get some sleep. I got one visit and they got the warden to allow me to go into regular population with the other country club inmates. I immediately was up in there ministering all up in the brothers faces the whole time. I got visits left and right.

The wife came kind of shook and nervous as a wreck. I was calm and held my Bible. It was my children seeing me behind that glass in the orange county jumper that got to me. I felt my daughter was too young for this place. This was the wife who up and left because she wasn't happy. She was trying to attend the function in Texas I didn't arrive to and I was in the middle of this incident. I told her that if the promoter admitted her to come fine with him. I only was interested in only seeing my daughter there and not her. She and the kids left. Now here she is like she's concerned as if all the pretty words she gave the crowds in Texas about me "in trouble and couldn't appear!" I couldn't talk about the clients and the case. This made her angry as someone else was in her head too.

16

VIP Limo

All kinds of people like the bails bondsmen assisted me and explained, "Leave your wife, she is not for you!" I didn't understand why my wife was so angry. Neither did my bosses. At first, it was told to me it was because she couldn't receive my property: my car, my wallet, my keys, and credit cards. She eventually got into our home, or at least her dad did. I had called and given her mother, Lucille, all the full instructions of how to enter the property. I had made provisions for each current situation now that I knew there was one involving me. I think some trusted people pissed off the wife a bit too much and won't admit it. I was in a real bind and everybody thought that lady is not your wife and once you get out on bail, really it's your choice, but divorce her buddy! She abandoned you once again when you needed her the most!

All those people were right and I didn't do this to her when she came to Colorado and needed help and even church people were avoiding her every time in her situations. Thank God my bosses and client took care of me those six to seven months that I was on bail. (One boss even wrote a huge IRS claim of $14K that I never received in anyway.) It was a hard pill to swallow. People will screw you over when you are down.

What took the cake was that every time the bondswoman dealt with the wife, I was told she was acting weird. The bondswoman and her husband didn't have to lie. Before I got out I was told to call the house. She'd then fuss at me for not calling her. I told her that I had no problem calling her parents home. Why I didn't call our house? I had the number changed. So I really had a lot on my plate. Together she and I could've conquered the world. Or so I thought.

17

Out on Bail

While on bail I partied with celebrities, wore clothes straight off department store racks that arrived by limo because I couldn't go home. I paid everybody for everything and favors as I kept good track of every deed done and gestures of good will. I met the men who paid half of my bail. They heard how as a minister in county jail I conducted my self ministering. They wanted to thank me for keeping them out of trouble and protecting their families.

At the Tulsa / Muskogee / Muskogee All Black Rodeo, I was speechless standing in front of six to seven men draped in platinum. I was informed of who my next clients flying in for concerts would be. I proceeded with them to attempt to enjoy the crowds and events to my amazement like a real country cowboy. I knew once again that I could not put my client's relative on the stand for my defense on trial. Even the mother tried this with detectives while I was locked up. Anyone who came to my defense was chased off with threats of confinement. Now that's a foul person in the justice system, period. I'm told that they took her testimony of domestic violence on tape and then threaten her to shut up or she'd face charges.

In the same way, my court transcripts were said to have been unclear and incomplete. Some people only see the constitution as an illusion of rights to others.

Later, while fulfilling my community service hours, I maintained composure. The student kept running away from home. The body count in the streets escalated as I warned officials. The student was afraid she would be put on the witness stand. "Why does Mr. Mike have to get in trouble? He's the one who only tried to help us!"

My ex-wife just didn't understand. Rev. Kelly in Denver once said all this to me on the slide: "This gang and street intervention stuff can cost you your family, even if it's a hard ministry work." Many feel that Reverend is a fake, but I know better though I've heard lots of sad things unfortunately. Telling my own story maybe can help someone else. My fall has to benefit somebody, I pray. I kept praying for strength while I still had to monitor the client's safety as agreed at the rodeo. The DA's office kept getting calls now that me and dude's wife were and item and all sorts of put him under the jail propaganda. You know it's all true when someone in the DA's office comes and tells you the same things going on. They didn't have to, but they had a good reason for providing the behind the confederate lines, details that may save another African American now a pawn in their game. It wasn't the person's job or business to get in touch with me as I was interviewed on the radio he heard of the OU hit song I was working on, We Took the Trophy.

One of my clients arrived. I was on the clock again. We went to eat with the promoter when he announced who I was working as bodyguard for. It was my ex-wife's cousin's former sister-in-law, Yolanda Adams. Yolanda's brother was married to Cindy's cousin and it was a bad divorce. While in her hotel room, she explained this to me. Yolanda was being supported on tour by AJ a music minister from Florida who went to college with me at FMC- Florida Memorial University. We all laughed and tripped out hard. The promoter was shocked too. Later, back-to-back were Charlie Wilson and the GAP Band, after Snoop Dogg and DAZ, plus a few others into my hearings and sentencing. I stayed busy even on bail securing my clients.

18

Attempted Murder Was the Case

I was told: "They want blood. You are an African American. Take the plea and get probation. Mike, let's deal very lightly with this. Your wife is also trying to put a protective order out against you since we didn't tell her if you were out or not." I had ties to the courthouse since I was their top officer securing jurors and judges safety daily with the sheriff's department prior to all of this. I asked for a non-profit sector to do my hours at the Salvation Army on Denver Avenue. Later, these things were used against me. I knew the courthouse was a trick off community service site and my other civilian work post I sued for a undisclosed amount with hip-hop. The Supreme Court case gave $9.5millions to the Florida case for Adam's Mark Hotel. I got a few grand that kept me well cared for thanks to a good friend of a friend and Attorney Goodwin as the story previously ran also on the cover of his newspaper the Oklahoma Eagle News. The hotel gave me hush money and I received the other difference during my sentencing. Amen.

19

The Night Aaliyah Died

I can't remember this slim bright-skin singer who always wanted me to be his bodyguard and kept saying it as all the girls would just mob him. He was shocked. I knew who he was with all his wealth and lavish lifestyle. I'd still helped him out when I was with others and then with Nelly on another date. Just can't recall his name.

I was pretty intense that night in Oklahoma City. I had strict client instructions: don't shake hands, smile, or talk. This was the night the singer Aaliyah's plane went down. Brandy and Ray J's mother, Sonya, was on the phone to confirm the tragedy. I called my sister Toni in Miami, who lived near the flight's departure airport on Pembroke Road and University Boulevard. It was true. Radio program directors were reporting the story nationwide. I was asked to lead the prayer. We all agreed: there'd be no after party. When we returned home to our families, we told everyone that we loved them. It could have been us.

I didn't get to see my daughter on her birthday when I got back. I prepared everything for that visitation at Pastor Lewis

Bumpers' church as a third party of both parents in the temporary divorce papers that read that I would have "all communication means with the child." The judge was firm with the ex-wife and told her that he wanted "no problems" out of her and her mother. I sent the birthday cards to my own house where I had been paying the mortgage and had just paid it off from her family. Weekly, Gerald McMurray, my ex-wife's husband, called me with a warning: "Be careful, man, even if you have not done a thing. Be careful!" Later, I learned he was right on the money. Quietly a warrant was issued against me by her. This doesn't mention the cops being called on me when both lawyers and parties agreed to my removal of my property in the home. She'd leave and I'd bring the truck and lawyers would be there. Cops were called. I had to wait en route until it was all clear. Her lawyer was pissed off and told me how to get it over with. She quit the ex-wife in representation as we loaded the truck. People just like this and will stab you in the back. Later, I guess the birthday card was her last ditch effort to infect venom. Later after it all, it still didn't work. These were the things I faced while, on bail, on trial and incarcerated. Others will crap on you if you let them. I want it all to get out especially their names, where the truth will hit home.

20

3 Strikes

I didn't want to have Thanksgiving dinner with any of my clients, yet I was being invited. I sat all day alone before the next day of court. I would have to go before the judge again supposedly with no preliminary records, a new lawyer within the firm and not ask for a trial. All this already had the judge pissed off. I gave the DA the requested 100-page background report. I didn't hide anything. I didn't mean to be a sour poot, but the BET evening movie special that day was not good for me as reality set in: I could be going to prison for real. I sat and watched 3 Strikes with Snoop Dogg.

21

D.A. Carl Funderburk and Judge Linda Morrissey

The D.A. padded the sentencing with the victim's statement against me saying that he called my dad and that I lied about my life and ministry work. The D.A. lied on my dad saying: "He never knew about any of it." This was more information being padded in my case. My lawyer, a drunken OU Grad, showed up late to the sentencing. He was telling me to sign this crock of bull and believe me, I refused for a while. Even my name was spelled wrong, still to this day. He said, "You'll never see a day in prison." Standing there in my $600 suede dinner jacket and black slacks, that judge said what I had only heard in the movies.

She asked: "Are you sure you still don't want to testify, call witnesses, or get a trial? I can sentence you to 10 years in prison don't you know that? I responded, "Your Honor, I was in the line of duty protecting my clients and I can't put them on the stand."

This time as I stood before her, I gave my name. She called me a few things I'll mention later. I was immediately handcuffed. I asked if I could give my wallet to a friend who came to court with me. (Beverly would become my wife two years later). The judge said "no." The sheriff who cuffed me hard said: "Isn't this some crap! You had a license and you saved lives. Naw, I ain't cuffing you. Go ahead and speak with your friend." I grabbed my aching wrist and told Beverly where to look for a few hundred bucks in the wallet. She smiled. It was four hundred big ones. She screamed. The sheriff pitched a fit with other officers all the way to county lock up and that story spread and even changed the state's laws by the end of my sentencing in Oklahoma.

22

What Law Changed?
CLEET ! TITLE 21 § 1290.1

"If you are licensed armed you must have a private carry for use in the public off duty or in personal protection." The officer knew how we were trained and he knew the law as a few others in the same incident that year didn't meet my same fate and one guy shot the kid after the child left school threatening to return and kill. On return, he was wounded before he touched the property with only a cell phone in his pocket that got the bullet.

Tulsa School of Science and Technology, Tulsa, Oklahoma

Thursday, October 31, 2002 At about 3:00 p.m. this Halloween, a security guard, employed by Pinkerton/Burns Security, fired a shot at 18-year-old Jermaine Cox, a student who had been expelled for improperly touching a female. The security guard missed and the bullet hit another student as he left the school across the street. The events started at a nearby convenience store with an altercation by Jermaine who made a threat against the security guard. According to the guard, Jermaine reached into his pocket for a weapon and that is when the guard fired a shot. He missed his intended target and hit a 15-year-old male student. The bullet shattered the student's cell phone in his pocket and that a piece of the phone caused a superficial wound just under his eye. The wounded student was treated and released from the hospital. The Tulsa School of Science and Technology was formerly McLain High School in North Tulsa. www.keystosaferschools.com/.htm

10/31/02 Tulsa, OK—Details remain sketchy as the investigation continues into the shooting of a Tulsa high school student by a Security Guard. Early indications are that an armed Security Guard was attempting to shoot another student who may have had a weapon; however, he missed his intended target and accidentally shot another student across the street. The bullet apparently struck that student's mobile phone sending fragments into his face but not penetrating his body.

This incident has caused several agencies to look into the school's practice of contracting with a private firm to furnish armed Security Guards, the policies in place for use of deadly force, and the level of training specific to schools that is provided.

This shooting follows closely after a student shot his fellow student in New Jersey and a university student in Arizona shot and killed three professors before taking his own life. Tulsa Police are recommending that no charges be filed against the Security Guard involved in this incident. The Tulsa School District is reviewing its policy on training required of the Pinkerton Guards who provide security services for their campuses.

articles.cnn.com/2002-10-31/us/.shooting_1_security

I thought I was going to be sentenced to two years probation. After court I was ready to celebrate freedom. Like always entering county jail, I was kept on holding all day due to my security level, which as a former staff member, was flagged.

What and who a person is, is always consistent with their actions. This I keep repeating. I didn't forget what the judge fully said. It's branded in my head for life. And she was wrong. I knew she didn't know me or recognized me. I am the one who worked to protect her daily. I'm the one she supported that we search all purses, bags, and people through metal detectors. Her staff and a few other elites who thought their stuff didn't stink were trying to get me hammered on the job. It was Judge Morrissey who knew my security measures kept people like her, as well as other jurors and judges, from being killed.

23

M.T.S.

Now I'm the one you calling a menace to society! Three years in the ODOC! I was wounded inside and resistant with the peace that only came from God as I felt my spirit being crushed. I wanted to kick some butts. Why did God let this go down this way? I questioned. My clients were safe and alive and hey as you can perceive by now I needed a vacation from it all.

Wardon Von and I talked. We just sat and for a while we talked before I changed into the orange jumper. He reasoned that if I still worked for them he would have got me off. "We know you! This is politics!" I agreed with him, thinking about what that judge had said to me and about me. I knew the judges I knew and was affiliated with would eventually pull her coat tail or robe later on and thank God they did. This is all painful to write about, but I push on to bless the next person. I was often putting my butt on the line whenever they (The DA's office and juvenile courts) asked me to take liabilities by taking juveniles into my custody or be their court-appointed mentor. I use to receive life threats from families in the community. I was getting threats even while on trial because I guess others thought I was as vulnerable. On the church lot, I was set up and still opened a can of whip a** on this one vindictive juvenile's uncle and the courts backed me up as should've been in this matter. The judge didn't really know me and judges aren't perfect. Sometimes all they know is what the DA is pushing for and nothing of what the DA's holding back about the person's background or what's being fudged and padded. Some just see social and political status nothing else for a notch on their career belts. I had been telling Warden Von that if I worked in this place and they gave me the keys, I would let everybody go, free. "After correctional training taught me that when slavery ended the next day they started prisons, I resigned. Working in corrections is not for me as far as what I want to do." We both laughed, though he was sadden as most staff I met who read my files or got to know me. At the pay phone that night after sharing with the Warden, I gave my dad a call in booking. I let my dad know how the hearing went. "They threw the book at me pops," I'd said. You can be assured I told my dad of all that this DA and courts had said on record of his investigation of my background. My dad was very upset. I told my father that "it's okay," and that "I got my Bible … I'll be fine … I loved you."

24

Black Man's University

I really needed a break from some really toxic situations, including the soon-to-be ex-wife. Getting adjusted to jail or prison life takes time. I cried here and there, I guess, down the line. I had my moments of serious depression. I had to learn to stop isolating myself from others. My cell mates (cellies) were always cool. They all prepared me for the rodeo ride. Similar to my original booking, I went to church or chapel services every second I could. I was surprised by how all the previous news spread about the Bible studies and prayer groups on various pods or units we sparked them all through prayer and surrender in county jail at first. I learned who the others were behind these revivals on other units in county. It was Mac Franklin Alexander, a brother who was coming to me about how police were bothering him with petty stops in the community. Today Mac serves as a pastor in Denver and is featured on my Eulogy CD hit song, Where do we go From Here? He may endorse this writing as our testimony.

This all actually saved my life with my clients and their people. I had their respect and this was from guys I didn't even know. They were banned from the state for police shootouts.

They said that I "kept them out of trouble and they appreciated me for that. I kept them from doing something they had been waiting for years to do." I knew in a very real sense I had completed a very good work and a walk alone by total faith. In the eyes of even my closest family and friends, I had done a great injustice and wrongs. The word went before me that I "didn't belong there" as most inside did; that I had gotten caught up in the middle saving other people lives. When I eventually kept hearing this version almost near my release, I was surprised that so many knew my story and the truth about it all. This is what gives me the inspiration to share it today. I couldn't rat out my clients or endanger further their lives or my own. Even during the confession of a sin to a priest, crime is a scared matter. My mother told me often and I could hear her voice in that nine-by-fifteen cell: "You made your bed; you now gotta lay in it." Even the deceased has a way of speaking to you behind that fence and walls, believe me or you'll find out the hard way. Protecting me was not an issue. I remembered the wife saying during one of her visits before I obtained bail: "You said it. You said you were going to go to prison. You don't remember. Long ago that's what you said and spoke it into existence."

25

She Was Right

Yes, my ex-wife Cindy was right. I did speak my going to prison into existence because I felt it strongly at one time or another. I felt and saw that most Black males were either being killed or in jail, and that I was next. Even as a child, meeting men who had already gone or were in prison, women too, I made myself a promise. I vowed at a young age that if I ever went, what I would do, and who in my life I one day would model.

After many days I'd think about so much. I vowed to become like the Reverend Dr. Martin Luther King, Jr., and Malcolm X; to read every book, learn everything I could, and use my time to educate myself. On bail, after hanging out with the GAP Band and Mr. Charlie Wilson, I did something. I was really impressed to be asked to pray for them before they all hit the stage. Ronnie and I rode the limo most of the day as he dealt with Baby mamma drama, someone serving papers, the whole nine. What a time I had thanks to Dr. Leon Rollerson, a great mentor of us all, especially his brother to me. If only my childhood hommies could have seen me then. This was one of the groups I grew up on strongly in Miami. Because of the gap in my mouth, I was even teased as being the GAP Band.

It did affect my self esteem a little that was the dozens game played in the hood. Now here I was rolling with them on bail.

Now this is what I did. I took that first hotel check of buy out or pay off money and hit the road to Malcolm X's birthplace. I let the T-top down on my black fully loaded, chrome rimed, leather seated, four-door Eagle Dodge, popped in the new Charlie Wilson-CD Mr. Charlie, filled my gas tank and rode off, right up to Omaha. I had heard on Tom Joyner's radio show program how they were raising money for The Malcolm X Foundation, the saving of the property he was born on and where he saw his dad killed. I wanted to see this memorial site and I did. I presented a ministry sister whom I dearly loved, Lady J an Award for her music ministry. I toured the community with reporters and cameras in tow. I was so moved. It all prepared me to face many mistakes, choices and consequences. I buckled in for the ride of my life.

26

Rodeo Ryde and Killing Judges

While out on bail, I continued body-guarding. By accident while I was exiting the hotel a group of Mexican men were trying to drag a lady into their truck. I ended up rescuing her from an attempted kidnapping and rape. I followed them and called the Tulsa police, who later called Broken Arrow police. This was all by accident and over one night. The lady thanked me. I was later getting mail to come testify against the men. I told them I'd love to but where I was at that time would not allow it. My ship date to the main prison processing had been delayed another thirty days. No one knew why at first. I was eventually notified from the outside that while being inside the county jail, there was still a hold on me. I obviously had another hold for another court hearing and charges. My fake-lawyer visited and then told me to hire a free public defender. He's lucky they did cuff me for that visit. He was foul. He told me that I would only do six months and that the judge will file a review of my file. I would do the rest of my time on probation. He lied. I now know why they sometimes chain you at the feet and one arm to the table like on some visits in person. I needed to really spank this man up side his head with a brick. I arrived to court and a Tulsa University paralegal student from the Public Defenders Office reviewed my charges. She said, "We'll have to have them drop this. We have the birthday card you sent your daughter. You did nothing offensive and the judge allowed you to communicate with your child by all means. It's on the court's record of temporary divorce order. We couldn't find you and don't know how you even got into custody. This was a traffic warrant for pick up. Nobody knew you were sentenced nor inside here." She returned again and said: "The D.A. wants to drop it, but you have a violent charge already. He doesn't wanna kick a man when he's already down." I thought, okay. This is what the wife is doing and I have never ever done nothing directly to her, kicking me while 'em down.

I couldn't believe the judge I was about to go before. How did she get from juvenile court to this place? Before she was standing in as a judge sub, now it's a regular thing. Here was God, again. She had already heard the protective order matter on this other man, a relative of a client of whom she gave me custody. He was the man from the Full Gospel Church lot fight who attacked me and got knots on his head, huge ones too. This was the day I ruined my silk suit from the MC Hammer Tour. I had brought the child back to juvenile because of his life-threatening relatives. I was still made to take the child back regardless of the risk in assisting the courts and the child's rights. I was always clear and this judge knew it if the threat was on my life what I'd do as trained to protect others. He knew as I told her on this incident in her courts before. "I'd use the weapon I carry if he attempted anything else after his bold threats and now attack." She handled that. Like most, this dude was using the fact that I was out on bail to do what the wife and others was already doing to me. The judge straightened that out. Now here I was, in violation of a protective order against the wife and the evidence as bold as day, a birthday card. Something I had court permission to do by mail and phone to my child, also visitation. When the judge looked down now and saw AWDW (Assault With A Dangerous Weapon), three years, she screamed and jumped up and down, again. "Do you see why people want to kill judges?" She ran off the stand into her chambers. She had the bailiff flag down a female attorney who had just exited the court room. It took a minute in wait. She told her, "Sharon Ashe, give him your card. See that he returns from all of these charges. Something dismissed / suspended. The protective order ran concurrent with other charges." I exited with the rest of the shackled inmates as usual after the hearing, pulling chains back to county. Prior to leaving, I told the judge that I still need that robe for my album cover. She instructed me where to get it. I considered her my judge momma. She was a Christian who always made me represent with my rhymes of Jesus and the Gospel before I took kids into my custody in the past 1998–2001, few understood. (This is another story in my Autobiography I'm Not A Star).

Now I can start my vacation. Now don't you think the guards, inmates, and court staff told others what they had just witnessed in court. This is why I had to, six to seven years later, painfully tell it all and especially warn some while this is also therapy for me too, in getting it all out.

It was time for me to consider my scheduled times and what my routines would be as a Christian minister and then-inmate. All my time would be spent in books. I wasn't going anywhere any time soon. Riots or escape meant they were entitled to kill you on sight. It's true. In the New Testament, the former Roman soldier Saul, who became Apostle Paul, explains it twice.

Paul and Silas were locked up and the Angel came and freed them. The jailer saw they were gone. He couldn't kill them for escape. Paul had stopped him from killing himself. The guard and his whole family were saved, converted to Christianity, and as a result became Christians in *Acts 16:22-34(NIV)*. Later, they were transporting Apostle Paul, a former Roman hit man. Paul use to kill Christians by decree of the Roman leaders. Once he was converted and became a radical Christian. He was pullin' chains when they became ship wreck. Immediately the guards plan was to kill the prisoners before they tried to escape *Acts 27:42* (NIV).

27

Vacation vs. State Property

Freedom is a privilege. There are rules and procedures in place to deal with every situation a prison or a prisoner will encounter. Tear gas is held in the ceilings. Forget that they are only water sprinklers. One button and you are in a real gas chamber. This is a system that it's not really about the crime alone as much as it's about the time you get these days. It's about a profit and the private prison industry expansion. You play a role or part in the legal or justice system's bottom line. Enough books are written on this. Pick one up and read it. In fact, read them so you will keep your butt out of these places of slavery. Forget rehabilitation in there. You have to choose to do that for yourself, period. That's the reason I'm sent back to society to tell you. That's the real reason I'm writing and speaking and warning you. Do not go there accept to visit our brothers. These are the things that the prison system does not want you to know about and how they operate. I told my daughter today this morning what Daddy was doing. She's ten going on sixty as I write this. She says to her mother, an author, "Mommy, this is what Daddy is doing. He's writing a book about how he went to prison and how it was for him … Mommy, he wants to stop people from going to jail and prison." I'm proud of her and her writing works and her journalism degree from OSU. I also saw how she used that education against me. I'm an artist slash activist and educator, period.

My daughter continued: "Daddy, be sure my brother Mikey reads it so he will never go to prison, ever, Daddy!!!" She had no clue of how much I've drilled this into his and other young people's heads so often since my incarceration.

28

Them, You, and Me: Public View of Prison(s)

I have helped to secure many careers for college students and friends in the field of corrections. Through ministry, and prior to my case, I've visited many prison yards and camps for years. Wardens have eaten with me, met with me entering their facilities. Now I'm being processed into the Oklahoma Department of Corrections. I have a real glimpse of all this rollout, pulling chains is sometimes seen in the movies the way it really is. Consider the movies Penitentiary, Con Air, First Felon, LIFE, Hurricane, and Redemption. You are not exactly told all the logistics only to get ready. You better believe that you're lucky if you take anything with you. No extra clothing, and a lot of other stuff, unless allowed. Believe me its basic essentials only when pullin' chains. You won't see most of what you do carry in pillow case or nap sack. No mail, no regular meals and a lot of behind: butt cheek checks. Butt naked you better spread your cheeks apart so they can look up into your cavities. County jail or prison, it's embarrassing. But that's not a word for it. It's beyond dehumanizing unless you get a kick out of looking up peoples crack side or allowing others to look or stick their fingers in yours. It just really depends. I ain't knocking nobody either. Choose your own ideology about all this. In pulling chains the buses get loaded with inmates, your already-chained legs are pad locked to the bus floor. Forget being comfortable. What if the bus flips over or catches fire and explodes before you get unchained or out? You have no rights. Wherever it flips is where you'll be hanging. You and those dogs chained in next to you aren't going anywhere. Oh, and I can't forget the guard holding the shotgun for "extra security" measures.

29

The Food, Cells, Smells, and Safety

You have just given up your life and human rights and they plan to make sure you know this. I thought the jail house meals were mudd and water most the time. Now the state food looked like dinner at your best friend's house at Christmas and it was good even if the chicken tasted like wood or rubber and was bleeding red or spoiled. You'll eventually eat or die from hunger. I chose to fast from it all for very good reasons. (Pullin' CHAINS) People are transported in groups or at sets at times. The green bologna is real, ask a fellow first. Prisons make most of their own food, especially everything at these state-run places that have their own farms. The bologna has been sitting in a barrel or a box, or wherever it's called, until it is served to you for that day. I passed it off or on and kept the little fruit dessert coconut grains, apples, or oranges. I'd trade you my sandwiches for like three white wax baggies of fruit grains. The holding cells inside before you are processed into prison can vary depending how the prison is set up. This one thing doesn't change: it's huge, cold, or dirty. And you can trust this. No joke. That blankety-blank toilet is going to be full of crap. Those who ate the green or almost brown bologna would start breaking wind and smelling like a dead rat or rotten dead dog or the sewer in the corner—fast and quick. The guys without tobacco or cigarettes or black and milds or alcohol or other drugs, are fiendish for anything. I'd take the coconuts, climb the top bunk with no mattresses, or I'd get down on the floor underneath the bottom bunk to sleep.

30

Don't Drop the Soap

Keeping your mouth closed will save you some teeth and a butt whipping, especially the young brothers and that's black or white. Respect yourself and others will, period. It's all about how you carry yourself. Being around these different men who are killers, criminals, and more will teach you a thing or two about life. It taught me a great deal.

One lesson was that you ain't nothing special up in here. You got a number and you are questionable, you do as you told and you do your own time. Don't let others trick you off or get you involved in their messes. I always watched people I showered with, or who I was near or around constantly. I was in the army. I played football from the 7th or 8th grade. I learned that you never know a man unless you are that man. Don't think it's a comedy line or joke. You better not drop that soap! Forget it being the wrong person, period! DON'T DROP THE SOAP. Handle your business.

31

Cutting Hair and Mental Test

At The Lexington Processing Center, I thought you all want us to cut our hair off? I said, "Hey sergeant, I did this in the army at boot camp. I'll chop all their hair off and fast." I became a prison barber on the spot and I did chop them fast. I must've cut seventy-five to 200 heads. They just kept coming and the word spread fast over the facilities. I had only been there for a few hours. My sister in law, Weorgia blessed me with a childhood gift-given talent that helped me as a barber and was now being put to use. I would only cut hair in the Tulsa-County jail for those who begged me or the cellmates. I wasn't being stuck up. You gotta know who to service and who not to, period. It's a right to choose. In processing into prison, you will be tested. I was given a TABE Test, locked down testing, no heat, and butt testing; no bath, shower, or change of clothes; food, mail, or phone calls. Your security level is being classified and you don't know it either: low, medium, or max, and that's included with your crime classification too.

I promise you, if you don't know the Lord Jesus Christ as your Savior who will protect you, eventually you will. You will call on Him if you are human and you are being dehumanized and mistreated. You gonna call your Creator. I had to be levelheaded and endure and pray the prayer of faith, often. I had to have more courage and confidence. I kept getting nothing but blessings but they didn't come without tests. God told me that I "needed to be levelheaded for others not just myself. Provide all the spiritually missing pieces to these men at all times." This is who I am a minister and nothing changes that not even this tough love language that may have some tactless brassy choice words of profanity. My French is one way to convey a serious point for those that relate to that. I know what the popular holy than thou are saying the whole way. Maybe this isn't for you so judge me as you choose. I don't claim perfection, but I will be effective. Anyway, those that behaved went on to other facilities and faster and those who went crazy or couldn't pull it together. They stayed on serious thirty- to sixty-day locked downs in a cell 24/7. These fools started a riot more than once. They flooded the toilet onto the floors. A racist guard really worked us up; giving us no heat in the cold temperatures and feeding us nor allowing us to bathe and over for days daily. I labeled her the guard from hell. Word got around fast if I tagged you. It turned out that she was friends with one of the inmate's mother and family. We were mentally pushed to the brink of no return. It was real conditioning. How could one take a TABE test and score decent. I did like a one percent that I had to do over a year later to get permission to study law. One half of the math was so high they made me stop taking the test and sent me to my unit in 2003 before release. In processing, it was like we went days on end locked down as if they were short staff or just plain forgot about us. It turns out it was both. I was always paired with veteran inmates who knew how to do their time inside. I still couldn't believe that they were snatching the pages out of the Bible with no ink to smoke tobacco. I was immediately dubbed "the Rev." I didn't care either. Once the riot was almost over, we were let out for food only sometimes. Top brass men came by. I got up out of my seat in chow to tell them what the matter was. I asked, "Hey, what are you going to do about all this?" I knew Satan wanted to take us all out. I knew that I had to be a doer of the word of God and be a new leader of leadership. They were making us real inmates, but my response was that I am a child of God, an awesome God. Don't rejoice over me O' my enemy. Though I fall I will rise; Though I dwell in darkness, the Lord is a light for me. (Micah 7:8)

32

Introduction to Me

All the inmates listened quietly as the water was leaking down floor to floor. It was serious, I am telling you. Any wrong move can mean a man's life-literally. I learned later the brass was there also just transporting this huge brother, Big Will, who had whipped the butts of seven or eight cops. He looked it too. He was sitting there in street clothes torn during our chow time. Later down the line like most he reminded me what he observed about me. He later was my Hodgen cellmate, weighing about 400 pounds. He explained more of this scene to me than I envisioned as a child. He had my back.

People were taking and trading food. I gave my tray away all the time. I was fasting and scared of the crap that was being dished out that was called food such as a pink and red chicken leg quarter or a fried pork chop. Now you gotta let me get that chop, let me at it. We gonna fight for the chop doc or who wants my dessert?

33

All Eyes on Me: Life File

Everybody around me was studying me. I rarely spoke a word and when I did, they listened. If you were foul, you'd get checked quickly. Being gay, a rapist, or molesters and more somebody's gonna get with you to make you bleed. If you viewed foul you will get beat out. Don't let the news describe a case of what you did and you are in arm's reach. You are getting beat out or killed. It's that simple. I helped save a lot of lives especially in high profile cases. You might wanna pray you didn't offend relatives of somebody's on the inside and they came across you or a guard exposes your charges.

I don't feel comfortable writing all of this at all. Like in the music business or the legal system, people don't want others or you telling all that goes on behind the scenes nor do they want to put it out there in the lime light. Many prison staff or caseworkers who read my file that the DA's office in Tulsa and Community Sentencing/ Probation people investigated then hid from the judge in my case. They had the prison people on staff pissed about this injustice.

I learned some like (Gary Anderson) knew my Florida classmates in college (Louisville) and in the professional sports (New England Patriots). Some knew my ministry mentors and boys club team members in Miami. They'd tell me to "be quiet and lay back, do your time and don't draw attention to yourself or files. We've been doing this too long of a time. We know who belongs here and who don't. Mike you can't save the world, man. You like my little brother. When you get out of here—okay! We got your whole life file here. You don't belong here."

34

Em' O.G. Now

My mind was swimming upon entry and this lady throws us all on my pod in a room and gives us this TABE test. She was nuts. I was drained from cutting hair. My brain was truly dead. I said how I scored and why I needed to be retested. I often insisted with staff and committees that I needed another trade and skills. I was told that my time was too short; that I was not qualified for state programs. I wanted to use my time wisely. I got the jobs other inmates laughed at and no one really wanted as janitor, tool room attendant, maintenance staff, or administration. It's all on my prison file.

Most post or assignments I worked provided me freedom unimagined. Trust me when I say freedom unimagined. Things and stories, I grew up hearing about from my godfathers, former drug king pens in Miami who later taught me to keep on reading my Bible. I learned all of it was so true, so I kept a leg up on a lot. Everybody knew what I did as far as work cleaning and church, reading at night also doing what I am doing now writing letters or poems. I wrote letters for inmates and poetry for their letters, often to make extra money.

A man who used to live in Miami whose aunt turns out to truly be a really powerful Black female judge in Oklahoma's judicial history connected with me. I had to check Gallimore's story out in the law library and it was true. People can tell their own lies too. He made sure I went to the law library. He made sure that I saw all the Miami and Trina videos on his privileged level four or five status. We had the same charges, but he shot the dude. I didn't. He was sentenced to ten years. I got a tiny three. I was always told to "Lay down, you going home real soon." Navy Officer Gallimore asked me to reach the kids. "Stop them from coming here, into the system!" I may be writing for a lot of you and myself but, it's for guys like this that helped me remember to make a difference with my life, that I score this work for also. They encouraged me and I feel I owe these men for their insight when I couldn't see in front of my own self physically. Gallimore should be released by now. I've tried at one point or another to reach his relatives directly since my release. I am grateful and they do know this. You could tell who the youngsters were that had to fight, wound, and witnessed lots of knives, blood, and had been around death. You could feel who was lying and who was really warning you and I hope that's what is happening here. You see, this is one man's experiences and journey and heeding, the warning to stay your butt out of prison. All I can say for those who just think this is a good read while you doing your time. Or what can I tell you, you don't already know? What I do know is God above on high was watching over me and can you say the same for yourself and if not I can help you with that there. No problem—I know I got the Holy Ghost hook-up with my father the OG of OG'z maker of all creation, my daddy, almighty GOD.

My first day inside the big house was a medium yard (1/17/2002), James Crabtree in Helena, Oklahoma. I was shipped across the state of Oklahoma almost near Kansas. It was Dr. King's birthday. The inmates were going to have a Kwanzaa / Dr. King program after chow. I needed to be here for this. I eventually was allowed to mix with the medium security's inmates. I couldn't eat the food, although I did try.

I had a Salisbury steak or meatloaf slice wrapped in foil. I took one bite and there was a huge fingernail or toenail in it. I took it to the head kitchen manager. We quickly became acquainted. This was the night, he downplayed the whole thing. How could this happen? I was really hungry too after coming to a new yard and pullin' chains from Lexington. This is prison life. On January 17, 2002, the program in the gym started as hundreds of inmates from everywhere stood around as I glanced from up front like it was church or an NBA game. I began to cry before the actual program started. I thought of our ancestors and all they had sacrificed their lives for our freedom. I had surrendered my freedom back to the white man's system. We had all fallen from grace. We all stood to pray and all joined hands. I walked over to this one man they said was one of the wardens and their staff table of four. I joined hands with them and the whole place, we prayed. I was the only one, a new inmate, this was probably a no-no, but I did it. Nobody told me this was one wrong move could get you killed, aiight. God had allowed me to do that. Every inmate I guess had heard all about what this new guy had done. I was being dubbed "Rev. and Malcolm X at Lexington." At Crabtree they dubbed me "Church Boy."

35

Bo Jangling

Eventually, I was moved and shipped due to what was said about me having too much influences amongst or over inmates. Attorney Ashe soon found me, wrote, and then called. It was not good and I was about to be hidden again in transport/shipping (Pullin' Chains). I worked for the warden daily. I was called nightly after dinner and yard counts to the prison entrance. Everybody and inmates knew my name who heard a guard's radio. "Hey, send Pennington up here to drop the flag or raise it." Inmates on the medium side of the yard would say how it sounded to the youngsters who were inmates. "You are like them there old dudes, Bo jangling for the man. "Yes, yes, sir! No, no, sir!" I knew what he meant, but as they found out later, I didn't play that. When I complained with inmate Robert W. Gallimore how he was being treated in visiting and everything about his ill mother. I got really on the crap list of a few. I got really targeted by the top bosses or guards. This got every inmate and staff so pissed off. Some staff even quit their jobs after being there eighteen to twenty years, basically retired. My former Tulsa boss, Mike Heath, wrote the facility requesting that they have me sign an affidavit to release his company-issued .357 from Tulsa Police Department's property. I was already being considered to work with the Lifer's Program, talking to teens who would tour the prisons. What I didn't know was that some would kill to have this privilege. They never knew who referred me to the program. There was a guard who used to tease me, or so he thought. He'd say: "tell me how you used to slap them whores around ... how much are you balling and slinging rocks on the outside." This white boy was out of touch and always had something to joke about. I rarely responded. I'd only do so while retrieving and folding the flag during the evenings. My reply would always be, "Naw man, not me. I'm not the one. I don't do that. I once did, but I love God. My momma would turn over in her grave." I was told he wanted me to buddy up to him so I could grab the dope from the outside cans and bring it on the inside. The officer, Michael Shelite, pulled me out of church and tested me for drugs I'd never ever seen. I lost ninety days due to a false positive. People lost jobs. I went off and wrote their superiors and won my case. My days were never returned.

I stood up to make a difference after inmate Gallimore was being harassed. I was now catching the heat for being a witness. People don't know how serious it was about to be—a real prison riot. It's not good when prison staff or a guard start gunning for you or riding somebody for no legitimate reason. That's a real dirty game.

36

Historical University Research

I got pulled out of church and was tested for drugs. I stood in line. I observed the ways in which a crack-head inmate serving eighty years was acting. He said, "Let me get some water. I'll go first." I sat down since the line was long. Some guards from Gallimore's situation were closing in and doing the testing. I held a shiny gold and red book about Egypt and the pyramids on my lap. I always kept books with me. A brass officer walked up and asked to see it. "Are you reading this?" he asked.

I answered, "I am." I was paying more attention to his staff and what was about to go down. I was the last one to test. I first asked not to be tested by Shelite as it was a conflict of interest. I was still made to be tested by him. I whipped out my private to give them urine right there. They backed up and asked me to go to the restroom with a cup. I came back and watched them chastise me with an alleged dirty drug test. I said "Whatever! If you find something in my urine, it's Psalms and Proverbs."

I went to my unit and told the lady staff on duty Mrs. Dooley. She said, "I sent you to church and the whole yard was locked down for this. You don't do drugs. No!" She rose to her feet, stood behind me, and cried. It was count time again and I wasn't even asked to stand by my buck. I sat in the day area in total shock. All the inmates, especially the ones who watched me all the time, said it again as I entered our unit the first time. "Hell naw!!! Church Boy ain't doing no drugs." My whole unit told the rest of the yard. I had support and love from people I didn't even know knew me or that somebody cared. They did my legal briefs through those that owed huge prison debts or owed others who sent me to them. Everybody, including staff, came together on my behalf. I was sent to staff for a court hearing preparation. My other case manager laughed and raised hell. She walked and talked and had me follow her around the buildings of the prison yard. She told me, "You go. Tell them I said that I ain't coming! I know what they doing. I'll take care of that. I know what they are doing I'll take care that. It's bull****!"

There were others in the executive staff that played dumb and I was feeling numb. Eventually, Warden Jordan, for whom I worked, and another warden who made me sign my weapon release to Mike Heath Security & Investigations, responded. I was just about to be approved for the LIFERS Program's involvement. So many turned sissy on me, again. The one case manager who did go to court with me was so funny and cool. On the first round, he stepped outside to smoke a cigarette. Mr. Grogen said, "I gave you copies of that 100-page life file for the LIFERS Program. The one the DA's office and probation in Tulsa County hid from the judge in your files like your licensed weapon in the police department's property never mentioned until now. Your civilian boss is asking for it back from police. I researched you and you shouldn't be here son, in prison." I looked hard at Mr. Grogen and said back to him,

"I know and my celly got it from you and showed everyone and all the inmates now want autographs." I didn't know staff had the file at first. For months as my boss was contacting them. They were checking me out fully. I didn't know anything. Grogen hit his cigarette and said, "You are good like a preacher with a sermon. You were very good in there." We were asked to step outside. I ruined the case.

God told me all the staff was in trouble and that were being busted down and it didn't help that one day. I chased a prison task force crew of politicians down and spoke up to the regional director visiting at dinner with a committee on the prison yard. I went outside one night and I thought they busted Shelite down in rank. He was dumping trash and checking doors. I said, "Man, hey man. God told me to pray for you and your family." It was the night before the final hearing. He came over in the dark and said, "Hey, you are going to pray for me and my family?" I said, "Yep!" "They made me do it," he confessed. "They put me up to it. I work over nights now. Tell them to call me at home. I will drop everything and these charges. The test wasn't real." I thought oops. Oh my Lord, I can't believe this! By then I had told the kangaroo court hearing officer: "If I'm doing dope, PCP, and Meth, Ray Charles could see it. This wouldn't require a test, period." We had had each drug broken down and its chemicals on paper, cited statutes, and the manufacture's procedures from the test and the manual's instructions for administrating the test. It turned out Shelite had also done the paperwork incorrectly. This was a reenactment of my gun or weapon charges padded and fake. Glenn Sheppard (singer, Helen Baylor's cousin) was my "quiet" Johnny Cochran. That's how he described himself all the time. Thanks everybody, and Shep. His cousin had been instrumental in me getting started in music ministry in church in Miami at New Way Fellowship in the 90s after my college and 2 Live Crew running days. She stood up and spoke my very purpose in which I've wrote to you about earlier. She was the one who told the church to let me go and how full of God I was to reach the communities. After she spoke that, I ended up in Los Angeles with the gangs and met Gospel Gangstaz whom as a result of this prison bout I relate much better to their journey as former Crips and Bloods in Ministry. We met in Watts, but after that they would come to the Set of Arsenio Hall Show and bring me their music and I promoted them. They rose so high on the music charts and this was way before my AWDA charge I was at the Stellars to support them and ended up on the show's filming getting my praise boogie on as God told me to "dance like David danced" at the end of 2000.

To all of you guys, I thank you and Gallimore including the staff, all of you who had my back. I thank you and love you. I had told the hearing officer that if I am doing any dope or drugs, everybody is doing drugs. "It's in the kitchen, it's in the food, and it's in the water. Everybody's bringing it in and doing drugs!" They were so ticked off and pissed at Shelite for doing the right thing. This could be one reason why he was awarded in 2008 Security's Supervisor of the Year over all ODOC Facilities. He did the right thing. This is how one can be disciplined by staff. Today, I recognize that Michael Shelite now a Chief of Security in ODOC was only doing his job. He was honest and professional while being hard on us. I commend him for being a stand up---C.O.- Correctional Officer. We are in touch these days and now it's water under the bridge. I learned he's always treated offenders with respect and treated them the same. Let me state for the record he did help restore my confidence in the system. He was the villain at one point and looking back he saved my life as a result when he came forward about it all. My point was once you inside they can control your life and you're vulnerable. Stay out !!!!

My ninety days of good time were gone and never returned. I had to make sure every prison official had a copy of that case. It was suppose to make it into this book. Although, I was ignored at first, heads eventually rolled. I had no time for any of this. Not only did my sister die, but a very famous female I use to minister to died. Lisa 'Left Eye' Lopez from the group TLC was so talented and gone like my other clients Gerald LeVert, Tupac, Jam Master Jay, and Michael Jackson ... all gone too soon. I will never forget how when all this was going on at Crabtree, the attorney calling, my boss calling, the mess with staff going on. I will never forget how they responded learning my weapon I released to my boss's request was not the weapon I was charged with (grounds for appeal). They sang this all over the prison yard, especially the staff: "You didn't have a 9mm."

One lady on staff watched how I was treated for a minute daily and called me up to her office to share this one thing with me: "No matter what they do to you don't let it make you bitter." She worked for Warden Donnie who ate with me often. My jaws dropped. This lady also knew what was going on. Years later I learned that she began her position as a teen and that she experienced problems with the staff. I was told that she was attacked and abused badly. I later cherished her very words in all that you are reading. I tried my best here to not be bitter friend in nothing. Was I affected? You bet ya'! Did I stay strong? Sometimes I wonder.

I was not going home in six months with Attorney Ash checking up on me reporting this mess to the judge. But it did, I think, save my life. I was being shipped out of the way to a private prison in Lawton. They knew they wanted to kill me. I even believe the DA's office was in on it too. The lifer who made sure I didn't get in his program that was working to parole him. He never knew it was the Muslim lifer brothers that sent me to participate and guys from Tulsa who watched how he crossed me up with the guard Michael Shelite. We could've been tag team, toe-to-toe or back-to-back reaching kids together. Upon my words on exit they would do him up after count and stick this fool. We all gathered around him at breakfast to inform him we all knew what he did. He tried, but he couldn't explain anything. How could I take this fake Christian and Toastmaster speaker's life?

I told the brothers that it was up to them. I realized he was a foul two-faced Langton University graduate. I told him that I didn't want to hear his apologies. Everywhere was the same. I stood up for others and faced life threats from my own people, sometimes murder. I got the most respect on each prison yard I was ever on. It was God's favor over my life and nothing else. And I know it. All the young guys (crash dummies), sexually confused or gay guys, bangers, all the people staff sent to me to assist during my stay. I pray that I was of some help in Jesus name. You guys cracked me up before riots started saying that I spoke up for you all sounding like Democrats talking to Republicans. I got a lot of love from you guys. I lived my life before you as I did on the streets. Some I took to church. To some said, "I'd never come back to visit you guys." Well after this book is complete, here I come, again.

I was shipped to a private yard Lawton Wackenhut. Months later I learned about my sister Vicki's death. Apparently no one relayed my sister Toni's calls or any messages to me while I was at Crabtree. My family called and wrote and no one told me anything until I got my brother-in-law Kwame's sympathy card. It reached me and I called home in Florida. He's a veteran municipal law enforcement officer. Kwame is not only an educator and mentor, but his inspiration stands a lifetime of positivity with respect for the law and true justice. He gave me excellent advice on the best course of action when faced with criminal charges. I was sentenced in Tulsa, "the dust bowl." The place you "come to on vacation and leave on probation." That's a crime and a crying shame. Vicki was murdered in Miami and is still an unsolved homicide. I share other writings about her life as she asked me to. She always peeped what was being said about me in the family and would eventually come and pull my coattail on how to handle it. She would say: "Mike you kinda slow, but when you away from the family you do so well." She always offered keen insights into situations, but I shook off her input because of the pile of drugs we were sitting on. She was using, and I felt hurt about having to help raise her son when I was a teen myself. I think she had been in prison or on the run from the law for some time. But she was so giving that you couldn't hate her, and talented ... she could light up a room in a heartbeat. "Hey man, what it is? Come give your sister a hug, man." She'd always tell the story of how I tried to sell her for a dollar to a man one time as a kid. She believed in me and that I would be a successful entrepreneur because I was good at selling things. In Tulsa, I invited her in my home to be treated for AIDS and she got better. She praised the Lord and told me that she was ready to die, and why. I was prepared for her death, but I think her knowing I went to prison really was a downer for her. Each of my five sisters always protected me, and I them. I wish I could have stopped her from being found on the side of the Miami Airport naked and dead from an "alleged" hit and run accident. But I could not.

37

In Conclusion

Many said that I would be famous speaking over the world after my release. They said that I'd never write a book or become involved in organizations such as the Chuck Colson Prison Fellowship. Even one of the national headquarters directors of Charles Colson PF organization told me that I had a lot to prove with me "falling so far from God's grace." His words were salt in an open wound. Only Christians kill their wounded. I'm just glad my former pastor and friend, Dr. Tony Evans book God is up to Something Great was endorsed by Chuck. I made sure every clergy I knew in this country reached out to the guys behind the walls as Apostle Paul wrote letters in the bible's New Testament to the churches. This was major work for me to do the same to different church leaders while incarcerated.

I thank everyone including T.D. Jakes for allowing Michael Irvin and Deion Saunders to hit the states—facilities for Manpower that year. These NFL and Florida boys know me personally. It was no accident that Chuck Colson didn't see me for that program he brought to our Wackenhut Lawton Correctional. We had planned that function's visitation for months. I was placed and stuck back down in a pod area called the ghetto and it was really that, the GHETTO. Prison layout is important. You need to know where you are located at all times including geographically on the maps. One north end of the compound on S.E. Flower Mound Road in Lawton was called the Ghetto, a section of pods of the facility at Lawton. The assistant warden was still apologizing when I left because I enjoyed playing this game with him. Guards would come and do there like annual clean up of cell or lockers (a shakedown) and I'd be ready all year round. I would have so many books on Christianity, witnessing tracks, and just books in my cell. My locker was completely full. If a guard came to search my locker and search the books by pages, he'd get tired and saved evangelistically, and have to call for back up. The whole staff would be standing outside my cell door as I'd watch. Other inmates stood back. I'd pull up a chair right next to the director of security or wardens and we'd chat. When I asked the Warden why our unit in the Ghetto didn't get to come out to the presentation we organized it was a security type answer he gave me. What an apology about water, mud, and the rain serving only a select of the population. A lie! They are truly in control of you.

That was a media circus and buff job. I wanted to see Chuck! Pastor Evans sent all the guys in church a book through me and then Chuck who endorsed it shows up as a Warden of four Texas prisons and model programs. After The Water Gate, inmates said the same about inmate Charles Chuck Colson: "He'll never come back to visit us." I too fellows kept my word and have been going inside to facilities such as Radar Juvenile prison (months upon my release). Florida juvenile prisons not detention centers but, prisons. Now this is the book and public version. Too many assisted me inside those fences and every staff that stood up and righted wrongs when others sort to smash me out, I praise GOD for you. Thank you Mr. Joe Johnson, Ms. Black, Mrs. Dooley (retired), Mr. Dewey Patterson, who fought for my ninety days to be restored with no luck for my early release and the list is so long including Inmates. To my many strong prayer partners and the bodyguards who God sent so often as big brothers: Yes, I am still looking out and for you guys. I just can't seem to find you (Big Will and Scott). Get at me if you read this book. I'll give you a job. Much was excluded from these writings probably due to editing and grammatical challenges. Lastly I just got plain tired of rehashing how screwed up and stinking dirty games can mess up someone's life. That's the work of the devil himself. When it is in your power to do good and you don't, according to Proverbs, that's a sin under the color of the real law.

You can be sure that my vision for the next phase of reaching young people is not cut, edited, or whitewashed. I believe in having class, or, a big swagger, as they call it. Today you can be tactful and choose your words for various audiences as President Barack Obama does. Because we can all use the wrong words at the wrong time, even as President Obama has used the word stupidly. Get this no one is more of a pouf than George W. He was a plain dipstick. And I will never forget all the killings under his watch as Governor of Texas. Then there's also the California governor Arnold Schwarzenegger. I must reach out and keep going as to convey visually in movies and school plays for school children why they should never go to prison:

it's modern-day slavery!

I want children like my daughter and sons to read and know

each word in the United States Constitution and especially those written by Dr. King. I want them to know the Negro National Anthem, Lift Ev'ry Voice and Sing. My homeboys from Jacksonville, Florida wrote this song Lift Ev'ry Voice and Sing and moved to New York as I have now done in 2009 while finishing this writing. The teachers at Primary C Elementary made us stand and practice Lift Ev'ry Voice and Sing as if we were in a Broadway rehearsal.

Thank you for your letters and all who wrote to me. I saved them for years but lost many in 2006 in two storage units after giving up my homes. It's been a challenge coming back to the free world as it is called. It's therapy for me to write this book. Former Oklahoma State Congressman, Mr. Joe Johnson could probably have it in Congress or on the best sellers list. He's the relative of the writer, Mark Twain, by his mom or dad. Mr. J's New Directions entire class will probably tear it apart and praise the pages of truth as well as cry, as I have, in his class from the heavy doses of reality.

This book is for the betterment of programs like his and people that really want to help you rehabilitate. I pray that this program will flourish. I'd like to put this work into every inmate's hand. I didn't get jail house religion, oh, no. I got to see my own faith grow and really working and believe me it was tested, smashed, and melted.

Prior to my release, I went to work for Lawton Elgin County East Barn under County Commissioner Gail Turner and all his boys who loved on me. They fed me and did things that really helped to heal my heart and spirit, especially my supervisors Doug, Richard, and 'Ain't It'-Jim Bob, for whom I have a great respect. He'd have to tell his own story of the brutal attack that left him for dead. But he too survived and it's for men such as this (a real victim) that those who truly offend should live behind the walls and fences that have broke the law to whatever degree. Those prisoners are still human beings who suffer as continued victims. If we don't show them the way, who will? Jesus said: "Who is without sin cast the first stone?" Everyone dropped their bricks and rocks and when He turned to say: "Woman, where are your accusers?" They were all gone. On Tupac's release from Clinton Max, this young thug gangster said it best while banging on wax or CD's ONLY GOD CAN JUDGE ME !-----Tupac Shakur.

About the Author

Urban Christian Author Michael Pennington is an ordained minister and internationally known rap music pioneer. Music writer and producer, he is also a publisher member affiliated with BMI and ASCAP Music. His fifteen-plus year broad and varied career experiences include: public speaking and evangelism, hosting a syndicated radio program, public school educator, urban youth worker, and member of the Urban Church & Prison Chaplaincy ministries. As a distinguished rap minister and activist, Pennington has led the way of spiritual reformation in the music recording industry against gangsta-rap and lifestyles as an Urban Missionary under Compassion International in Denver Colorado. He continues to pioneer what has been dubbed Holy Hip-Hop music. He is the author of two books: Not a Star, an autobiography, and (Pullin' Chains) Stay Your butt out of Prison! Both are resource products of MVP –Press (Pennington Publishing House), which he found. As the Pastor of The Hip Hop Church of Denver, An Outreach of Reality Rap Ministries, Inc, it is his prayer that many lives will be changed as a result of his pain, struggles and triumphs.

Where Is the Author Today?

Upon release from incarceration on September 18, 2003, Michael returned to activism to improve prison conditions and restorative justice for inmates reentering society. The same year he made an appearance in the news on Oklahoma PBS TV news feature of the president's State of the Union Address. After becoming an owner of a couple of properties in Florida, he invested carefully until the damage of Hurricane Katrina and the housing bubble burst. He enrolled in a barber's college and made small strides until he graduated in 2011. Today he has returned to school to learn more about the law as an Academic Honor Student in Law. As president and CEO of Pennington Communications, Inc., Devine is continuing his goals of book publishing and speaking abroad on various topics including operating the Break Bread Prison Outreach Programs through 2016 as Pastor of The Hip Hop Church of Denver, An Outreach of Reality Rap Ministries, Inc. He also plans on petitioning the governor of Oklahoma for a pardon.

Strong, Empowering Scripture(s)

Acts 17:11 (NIV)
Now the Berean Jews were of more noble character than those in Thessalonica, for they received the message with great eagerness and examined the Scriptures every day to see if what Paul said was true.

Psalm 7:7 (NIV)
Let the assembled peoples gather around you, While you sit enthroned over them on high.

2 Timothy 4:8 (NIV)
Now there is in store for me the crown of righteousness, which the Lord, the righteous Judge, will award to me on that day—and not only to me, but also to all who have longed for his appearing.

1 John 4:8 (NIV)
Whoever does not love does not know God, because God is love.

Psalm 139:23-24 (NIV)
Search me, God, and know my heart;
Test me and know my anxious thoughts.
See if there is any offensive way in me,
And lead me in the way everlasting.

Ephesians 1:17-19 (NIV)
I keep asking that the God of our Lord Jesus Christ, the glorious Father, may give you the Spirit[a] of wisdom and revelation, so that you may know him better. I pray that the eyes of your heart may be enlightened in order that you may know the hope to which he has called you, the riches of his glorious inheritance in his holy people, and his incomparably great power for us who believe. That power is the same as the mighty strength.

Philippians 1:9-11(NIV)
And this is my prayer: that your love may abound more and more in knowledge and depth of insight, so that you may be able to discern what is best and may be pure and blameless for the day of Christ, 11 filled with the fruit of righteousness that comes through Jesus Christ—to the glory and praise of God.

Colossians 1:9-12 (NIV)
For this reason, since the day we heard about you, we have not stopped praying for you. We continually ask God to fill you

with the knowledge of his will through all the wisdom and understanding that the Spirit gives, [a] so that you may live a life worthy of the Lord and please him in every way: bearing fruit in every good work, growing in the knowledge of God, being strengthened with all power according to his glorious might so that you may have great endurance and patience, and giving joyful thanks to the Father, who has qualified you [b] to share in the inheritance of his holy people in the kingdom of light.

Ephesians 3:16-21

I pray that out of his glorious riches he may strengthen you with power through his Spirit in your inner being, 17 so that Christ may dwell in your hearts through faith. And I pray that you, being rooted and established in love, may have power, together with all the Lord's holy people, to grasp how wide and long and high and deep is the love of Christ, and to know this love that surpasses knowledge—that you may be filled to the measure of all the fullness of God. Now to him who is able to do immeasurably more than all we ask or imagine, according to his power that is at work within us, to him be glory in the church and in Christ Jesus throughout all generations, forever and ever! Amen.

Hebrews 4:16 (NIV)

Let us then approach God's throne of grace with confidence, so that we may receive mercy and find grace to help us in our time of need.

John 6:37 (NIV)

All those the Father gives me will come to me, and whoever comes to me I will never drive away.

Isaiah 43:25 (NIV)
"I, even I, am he who blots out your transgressions, for my own sake, and remembers your sins no more.

1 John 1:9 (NIV)
If we confess our sins, he is faithful and just and will forgive us our sins and purify us from all unrighteousness.

2 Corinthians 5:17 (NIV)
Therefore, if anyone is in Christ, the new creation has come: [a] the old has gone, the new is here!

Ephesians 6:10-18 (NIV)

THE ARMOR OF GOD

Finally, be strong in the Lord and in his mighty power. Put on the full armor of God, so that you can take your stand against the devil's schemes. For our struggle is not against flesh and blood, but against the rulers, against the authorities, against the powers of this dark world and against the spiritual forces of evil in the heavenly realms. Therefore put on the full armor of God, so that when the day of evil comes, you may be able to stand your ground, and after you have done everything, to stand. Stand firm then, with the belt of truth buckled around your waist, with the breastplate of righteousness in place, and with your feet fitted with the readiness that comes from the gospel of peace. In addition to all this, take up the shield of faith, with which you can extinguish all the flaming arrows of the evil one. Take the helmet of salvation and the sword of the Spirit, which is the word of God. And pray in the Spirit on all occasions with all kinds of prayers and requests. With this in mind, be alert and always keep on praying for all the Lord's people.

Lamentations 3:22-26 (NIV)
Because of the LORD's great love we are not consumed,
For his compassions never fail.
They are new every morning;
Great is your faithfulness.
I say to myself, "The LORD is my portion;
therefore I will wait for him."
The LORD is good to those whose hope is in him,
to the one who seeks him;
it is good to wait quietly
for the salvation of the LORD.

Matthew 11:28-30 (NIV)
"Come to me, all you who are weary and burdened, and I will give you rest. 29 Take my yoke upon you and learn from me, for I am gentle and humble in heart, and you will find rest for your souls. 30 For my yoke is easy and my burden is light."

Psalm 55:22 (NIV)
Cast your cares on the LORD
and he will sustain you;
he will never let the righteous be shaken.

Nehemiah 8:10(NIV)
Nehemiah said, "Go and enjoy choice food and sweet drinks, and send some to those who have nothing prepared. This day

is holy to our Lord. Do not grieve, for the joy of the LORD is your strength."

Isaiah 41:10(NIV)
So do not fear, for I am with you;
do not be dismayed, for I am your God.
I will strengthen you and help you;
I will uphold you with my righteous right hand.

Psalm 27:1(NIV)
The LORD is my light and my salvation—
whom shall I fear?
The LORD is the stronghold of my life—
of whom shall I be afraid?

Isaiah 53:4-5 (NIV)
Surely he took up our pain and bore our suffering,
yet we considered him punished by God,
stricken by him, and afflicted.
But he was pierced for our transgressions,
he was crushed for our iniquities;
the punishment that brought us peace was on him,
and by his wounds we are healed.

Matthew 8:16-17 (NIV)
When evening came, many who were demon-possessed were brought to him, and he drove out the spirits with a word and healed all the sick. 17 This was to fulfill what was spoken through the prophet Isaiah: "He took up our infirmities and bore our diseases."

Psalm 107:19-20 (NIV)

Then they cried to the LORD in their trouble,
and he saved them from their distress.
He sent out his word and healed them;
he rescued them from the grave.

Proverbs 3:7-8 (NIV)

Do not be wise in your own eyes;
fear the LORD and shun evil.
This will bring health to your body
and nourishment to your bones.

"All Inmates Should Be Given a Second Chance."

This caption and transcript editorial was made possible by R.R.M.

"All Inmates Should Be Given a Second Chance."

~ FORMER-PRESIDENT GEORGE W. BUSH

According to the Oklahoma Department of Corrections, there are more than 31,000 unemployed ex-offenders. This number does not take into account the former inmates not under their Department of Correction's supervision. A growing number say that they can't find work. How can former prisoners restore themselves after paying their debts to society? They need jobs to make a living once released from the system. OETA- Oklahoma Educational Television Authority's Royal Aills explains: "It often boils down to A CAN DO ATTITUDE."

"Only last week an employer, after four months of follow-ups, took a further interest in hiring me," he said. "He was interested in possibly hiring because I wasn't on drugs, seemed clean cut, appeared to have a brains and I came prepared."

Michael Pennington-Devine is an ex-prisoner looking for work. Formerly an armed bodyguard and CLEET security officer tasked with saving at-risk lives in an intense domestic dispute, Devine spent twenty months in prison on an assault with a dangerous weapon charge–a felony in Oklahoma. Since his release last September (over 130 days ago), he has been completing applications, attending workshops, and seeking out-of-town opportunities as well.

With rejection and negative responses, Devine disagrees, and he is not alone. On average, the Oklahoma Department of Corrections releases 500 inmates monthly.

Ron Skeen with Career Tech / State Employment Services helps many ex-offenders find work. On average he sees five to ten people each week, and reports that about 80 percent find work. "Many coming out of prison are still looking for what the employer can do for (offer) them. That isn't the job market anymore. Instead they need to be able to tell the employer what they themselves have to offer them that will make them want to take that second look at them."

For the twenty percent of Oklahoma's former inmates who are not getting that second look they say, "This America is not a land of a second chance, instead they say, it's a land of prejudice and fear."

This is why former-President Bush wanted to change that perception. During his State of the Union address on Jan. 21, 2004, he said: "All inmates should be given a second chance. So tonight, I propose to Congress a four-year, $300 million prisoner re-entry initiative to expand job training and placement services, to provide transitional housing, and to help newly released prisoners get mentoring including from faith-based groups."

"This is a process of elimination. It's sad that I have to use these kinds of words. My thing is that it goes back to this question: How are we really helping these people that have questionable or uncertain personal (discretionary) background situations?", says Devine.

For now Devine makes just enough (if any) money to get by. He says that his "pride has long since been left at the door," but he won't give up. He'll write his own ticket if need be with God's guidance. He's prepared to meet with the president shortly.

In Tulsa, for the Oklahoma News Report, Channel 11, I'm Royal Aills.

Career Tech says that "anyone looking for work can log on to their site www.oklahomajoblink.com there you'll find on average 130 jobs opportunities every week."

Recommended Reading List

The New Jim Crow, Michelle Alexander

Makes Me Wanna Holler: A Young Black Man in America, Nathan Mc Call

Miracle's Boys Jacqueline Woodson

I Beat the Odds: From Homelessness, to the Blind Side, and Beyond, Michael Oher

Fight the Power: Rap, Race, and Reality, Chuck D

The Isis Papers: The Keys to the Colors by Frances Cress Welsing(Dec 2004)

Think and Grow Rich: A Black Choice by Dennis Kimbro and Napoleon Hill(Sep 23, 1992)

Victory in Spiritual Warfare: Outfitting Yourself for the Battle by Tony Evans

Are Black Spiritually inferior to whites by Dr. Tony Evans

Raising Black Boys by Dr. Jawanza Kunjufu(Aug 1, 2007)

Marcus Garvey Life and Lessons: A Centennial Companion to the Marcus Garvey and Universal Negro Improvement Association... by Marcus Garvey, Robert A. Hill and Barbara Bair(Jun 2, 1988)

Street Soldier by Joseph Marshall(Apr 1, 1996)

Live from Death Row by Mumia Abu-Jamal and John Edgar Wideman(Jun 1, 1996)

The Classroom and the Cell: Conversations on Black Life in America by Mumia Abu-Jamal and Marc Lamont Hill(Dec 1, 2011)

Jailhouse Lawyers: Prisoners Defending Prisoners v. the USA by Mumia Abu-Jamal and Angela Y. Davis(Mar 1, 2009)

Visions for Black Men by Naim Akbar and Na'im Akbar(Dec 1, 1992)

Breaking the Chains of Psychological Slavery by Naim Akbar

(Jun 1, 1996)

Know Thyself by Na'im Akbar and Asa G. Hilliard III(Dec 1, 1998)

From Miseducation to Education by Na'Im Akbar(Jun 1983)

The Raising Him Alone Campaign announces its list of 30 Books for Parents raising a Black Male Child. The books selected inspire, challenge, confuse and stimulate the minds and hearts of parents raising boys in a "toxic" society.

The campaign realizes that raising a Black male child can be both rewarding but difficult. For this reason we are dedicated to supporting "Serious Parenting." Please share this list with others. Our sons are waiting for us to step up!

A Black Parent's Handbook to Educating Your Children (Outside of the Classroom) by Baruti K. Kafele

A Hand to Guide Me by Denzel Washington

Beating the Odds: Raising Academically Successful African American Males by Freeman A. Hrabowski, Kenneth I. Maton, and Geoffrey L. Greif

Cooked: From the Streets to the Stove, from Cocaine to Foie Gras by Jeff Henderson

How to Get Out of Debt: Get an a Credit Rating for Free Using the System I've Used Successfully With Thousands of Clients by Harrine Freeman

Kill Them Before They Grow: Misdiagnosis of African American Boys in American Classrooms by Michael Porter

Letters to Young Brothers by Hill Harper

Morning by Morning: How We Home-Schooled Our African-American Sons to the Ivy League by Paula Penn-Nabrit

Keeping Black Boys Out of Special Education by Jawanza Kunjufu

Raising Black Boys by Jawanza Kunjufu

Raising Cain: Protecting the Emotional Life of Boys by Dan Kindlon and Michael Thompson

Real Boys: Rescuing Our Sons from the Myths of Boyhood by William Pollack and Mary Pipher

Saving Our Sons by Marita Golden

Single Mamahood: Advice and Wisdom for the African-American Single Mother by Kelly Williams

Stickin' To, Watchin' Over, and Gettin' With: An African American Parent's Guide to Discipline by Howard Stevenson, Gwendolyn Davis & Saburah Abdul-Kabir

Strength for Their Journey: 5 Essential Disciplines African-American Parents Must Teach Their Children and Teens by Robert L. Johnson & Paulette Stanford

Tapping the Power Within: A Path to Self-Empowerment for Women by Iyanla Vanzant

The Black Male Handbook: A Blueprint for Life by Kevin Powell

The Bond: Three Young Men Learn to Forgive and Reconnect with Their Fathers by Sampson Davis, Rameck Hunt & George Jenkins

The Pact: Three Young Men Make a Promise and Fulfill a Dream by Sampson Davis, George Jenkins, Rameck Hunt, and Remeck Hunt

The Pursuit of Happyness by Chris Gardner

The Single Mom's Little Book of Wisdom by Cassandra Mack

The Warrior Method: A Parents' Guide to Rearing Healthy Black Boys by Raymond Winbush

Yesterday, I Cried: Celebrating the Lessons of Living and Loving by Iyanla Vanzant

Being a Black Man: At the Corner of Progress and Peril by Kevin Merida

Black Pain: It Just Looks Like We're Not Hurting by Terrie Williams

Boys Adrift: The Five Factors Driving the Growing Epidemic of Unmotivated Boys and Underachieving Young Men by Leonard Sax

Boys into Men: Raising Our African American Teenage Sons by Nancy Boyd-Franklin, Pamela A. Toussaint, and A. J. Franklin

101 Things Every Boy/Young Man of Color Should Know by LaMarr Darnell Shields

Come On People: On the Path from Victims to Victors by Bill Cosby

Behavior Changes For Success !

Now and in the future, winners will do the following things, **TO GUARANTEE SUCCESS** !

1. Make New Friends.
2. Have A Positive Attitude.
3. Attend Self-Help Meeting -- Support Groups - AA/NA.
4. Stay Employed.
5. Be Responsible -- Honest -- More Open.
6. Get Closer To Lord -- Church..
7. Have Personal Courtesy.
8. Have Personal Desire -- The Want To Change.
9. Accept Reality (Everything Is Exactly As It Is Supposed To Be).
10. Set And Work Toward Goals.
11. Strengthen Our Family.
12. Have A Mentor - Friend (Not A User) Sponsor.
13. Stay Sober.
14. Have An Exercise Program.
15. Practice Altruism - UCFO.
16. Correspond Or Communicate With ND Instructor.
17. Learn By Mistakes, As Well As By Mistakes Of Others.
18. Submit To Authority -- Enjoy Discipline.
19. Enjoy Life -- Have Fun.
20. Practice The Golden Rule.
21. Restitution -- According To Your Ability.
22. Constructively Fill Idle Time.
23. Further My Education.
24. Forgiveness -- Give And Get A Clean Sheet.
25. Improve My Personal Appearance -- Abandon Convict Habits.
26. Always Listen --Pay Attention, Give Heed.
27. Be Contrite -- Sincere Remorse For Any Wrongdoing --Repentance.
28. Think First, Act Second -- Not Act First, Then Think.
29. More positively control my Anger. (WON. HOWARD--AUG.'06)
30. Compassion and Communication with and for my Band of Brothers.

OKLAHOMA STATE DEPARTMENT OF CORRECTIONS - Consolidated Record Card

Victim Notification

DOC Number	DOC Reception Date	Gender	Race	Height	Weight	Hair	Right Eye
406740	01/11/2002	MALE	BLACK	6'0"	191 lbs	BLACK	BROWN

Name: PENNINGTON, MICHAEL J

SSN: — CSBI Number: — FBI Number: —

Alias Names and Additional SSN:
- DEVIN-PENNINGTON, MICHAEL J
- DEVINE, MICHAEL
- DEVINE-PENNINGTON, MICHAEL J
- DEVINE-PENNINGTON, MICHAEL VAUGHN

Date Of Birth: 09/19/1967 Victim Notification: NO Parole Eligibility: 09/2002

Religion: NON-DENOMINATIONAL

Skills: MUSICIAN

01/11/2002

Emergency Contact: — Contact Address: —
Telephone Number: —

CRF No.	Count	J&S Date	County of Prosecution	Offense Description	ETC	Sentences
2001-2037	1	11/27/2001	TULSA	ASSAULT WITH A DANGEROUS WEAPON	NO ETC	3 YR

Rule 8 Hearing w/in 10 days of release

Movement History From / To / Date	Classification/Job Action / Date	Charge	Disciplinary Record Code / Date	Punishment	Code
TUL/ LARC 01/11/2002	Initial Clsn 1/23/2002	Individual Disruptive Behavior 02-02-418 102	05 X 10 Days Loss 50 ECC	R.S A-2
LARC Recmm 1/23/02	Labor Pool 1/23/02			
JCF JHCC 12/18/02	Floyd Crofoman 2/1/02			
JHCC LCCC 6/24/03	Fired from Woodshed 9-30-02			
LCCC Dscn 9/15/03				

OMS00240

Oklahoma Department of Corrections
Document COPY

OKLAHOMA DEPARTMENT OF CORRECTIONS
CERTIFICATE OF RELEASE

THIS IS TO VERIFY THAT Michael J. Pennington , DOC # 406740
WAS RELEASED FROM CONFINEMENT AT Lawton CCC
ON THE 18th DAY OF September , 20 03 , AS A RESULT OF:

- [X] DISCHARGE, SENTENCE COMPLETED
- [ ] DISCHARGE, COMMUTATION
- [ ] DISCHARGE, COURT ORDERED
- [ ] PAROLE
- [ ] DISCHARGE TO PROBATION SUPERVISION
- [ ] APPEAL BOND/REVERSED AND REMANDED

Furthermore, that all applicable credits have been applied in conformity with statutes of the state of Oklahoma and established procedures of the Oklahoma Department of Corrections pursuant to case(s): **01-2037 Tulsa Co.**

- [X] Your field file reveals no required period of supervision with the Oklahoma Department of Corrections.
- [ ] Parole Date of Release
- [ ] Documentation in your field file reveals that you are under a term of (supervised) (unsupervised) probation pursuant to case(s) _____ until _____ . You are required to report for supervision within 72 hours (three days) to: _____

SIGNED THIS 18th DAY OF September , 20 03

Karen Coffman — Witness
Facility Head/District Supervisor/Designee

I HEREBY ACKNOWLEDGE RECEIPT: Michael Pennington 406740
Inmate's Name and DOC #

Inmate's Forwarding Address: c/o Michael Pennington
Reality Rap Youth Ministries, P.O. Box 50107, Tulsa, OK 74150-1017

STATE OF OKLAHOMA
OKLAHOMA DEPARTMENT OF CORRECTIONS
JIM E. HAMILTON CORRECTIONAL CENTER

LETTER OF COMPLETION

TO WHOM IT MAY CONCERN:

MICHAEL PENNINGTON successfully completed the following components of the Jim E. Hamilton Correctional Center New Directions Program.

Addictive Voice Recognition	20 hours
Overcoming Thinking Errors	30 hours
Rational Thinking and Stress Management	30 hours
Family Systems	30 hours
Substance Abuse Education	40 hours
Group Therapy	35 hours
Relationships and Parenting	40 hours
Assertiveness Training	20 hours

Successfully completed this 16th day of May, 2003.

Joe D. Johnson
Program Staff

Our teacher, we love, Mr. J,
  Seems to have plenty to say.

Fortunately, he's helped us to see,
  There's always a better way to be!

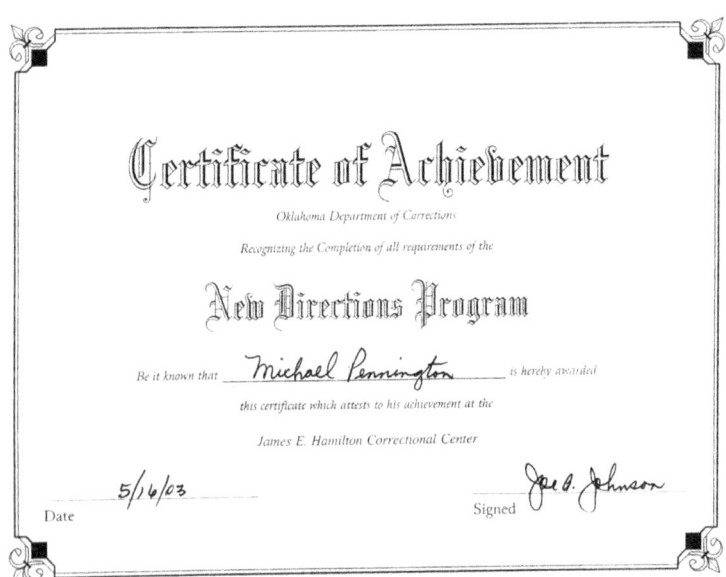

The Lord Reigns

By Michael Pennington aka Mike Devine

Psalm 93:1,The LORD reigns, he is robed in majesty; the LORD is robed in majesty and armed with strength; indeed, the world is established, firm and.

(Prayer) Lord Jesus help us this is my cry young people simply wonder and we don't know why. Sounds of terror in our ears. Distress and anger terrify our kids. Now they are settin' example of how man lives.

Verse 1
I met a young man running from the cops. He ran so much his mind couldn't stop. As I talked to the kid for a long time I couldn't help but to think that drugs destroyed his mind. I won't say his name, I hope it's okay movin' fast never thinking makes you go astray. The devil gives pleasure, let's you have a good time but at the end he brings pain and then it's Jesus time.

Once you get high you want it again but you have no more money for drugs my friend so you fake it and take it from someone you dearly love, drag'em through the mud to support ya buzz. Jesus with his mercy allowed man to win, over sin. Jesus died for the cause to be born again. (Jesus died gave his life for your sin).

Chorus:
The Lord Reigns, In Jesus you can make that change.
The Lord Reigns, Why does it seems so strange.
The Lord Reigns, Jesus cold runnin thangz

Verse 2
Jesus gave you a chance by puttin you in Jail so what's the decision heaven or hell??? After a few days you can bet you'll wake up in the night from a cold sweat(That's it).

Jesus why will be your call when you were chasin a fix not GOD at all. Put ya mind at ease pray and confess This is called repent now give GOD your best. Say Jesus I believe you the Son of GOD and when you died on the cross you did your part. Please come into my life make me a new creation. I'll read my bible and pray to you daily. Give me strength to obey the law and share this rhyme with another young brother !!

Chorus: Repeat

Verse 3
Now the change is deep inside your heart you gotta make it grow from the word of GOD. You know other Inmates, don't perpetrate you live. The light of Christ you must not hide. Your're livin in fear, study hard in GOD and every day you live, live wise for GOD. You wonder to ya self and through the bars you dream. Praying to GOD to be back on the scene. Now you there take a look around good. Where are the girls that be and the Boyz N the Hood? Now you may think Street

fast money is great. They are all dead. What was their mistake? Now your pockets are bare who cares? But, your soul is saved. You wake up from the dream so amazed elated that your name was not on the grave. GET SWAG- Saved With Amazin Grace. Get S-W-A-G !

www.ingramcontent.com/pod-product-compliance
Lightning Source LLC
Chambersburg PA
CBHW031630160426
43196CB00006B/354